OECD CENTRE FOR CO-OPERATION WITH NON-MEMBERS

Reviews of National Policies for Education

Estonia

OECD

ORGANISATION FOR ECONOMIC CO-OPERATION AND DEVELOPMENT

ORGANISATION FOR ECONOMIC CO-OPERATION AND DEVELOPMENT

Pursuant to Article 1 of the Convention signed in Paris on 14th December 1960, and which came into force on 30th September 1961, the Organisation for Economic Co-operation and Development (OECD) shall promote policies designed:

- to achieve the highest sustainable economic growth and employment and a rising standard of living in Member countries, while maintaining financial stability, and thus to contribute to the development of the world economy;
- to contribute to sound economic expansion in Member as well as non-member countries in the process of economic development; and
- to contribute to the expansion of world trade on a multilateral, non-discriminatory basis in accordance with international obligations.

The original Member countries of the OECD are Austria, Belgium, Canada, Denmark, France, Germany, Greece, Iceland, Ireland, Italy, Luxembourg, the Netherlands, Norway, Portugal, Spain, Sweden, Switzerland, Turkey, the United Kingdom and the United States. The following countries became Members subsequently through accession at the dates indicated hereafter: Japan (28th April 1964), Finland (28th January 1969), Australia (7th June 1971), New Zealand (29th May 1973), Mexico (18th May 1994), the Czech Republic (21st December 1995), Hungary (7th May 1996), Poland (22nd November 1996), Korea (12th December 1996) and the Slovak Republic (14h December 2000). The Commission of the European Communities takes part in the work of the OECD (Article 13 of the OECD Convention).

OECD CENTRE FOR CO-OPERATION WITH NON-MEMBERS

The OECD Centre for Co-operation with Non-Members (CCNM) promotes and co-ordinates OECD's policy dialogue and co-operation with economies outside the OECD area. The OECD currently maintains policy co-operation with approximately 70 non-Member economies.

The essence of CCNM co-operative programmes with non-Members is to make the rich and varied assets of the OECD available beyond its current Membership to interested non-Members. For example, the OECD's unique co-operative working methods that have been developed over many years; a stock of best practices across all areas of public policy experiences among Members; on-going policy dialogue among senior representatives from capitals, reinforced by reciprocal peer pressure; and the capacity to address interdisciplinary issues. All of this is supported by a rich historical database and strong analytical capacity within the Secretariat. Likewise, Member countries benefit from the exchange of experience with experts and officials from non-Member economies.

The CCNM's programmes cover the major policy areas of OECD expertise that are of mutual interest to non-Members. These include: economic monitoring, structural adjustment through sectoral policies, trade policy, international investment, financial sector reform, international taxation, environment, agriculture, labour market, education and social policy, as well as innovation and technological policy development

Publié en français sous le titre :
EXAMENS DES POLITIQUES NATIONALES D'ÉDUCATION
Estonie

Foreword

The transition of Estonia towards a pluralistic democracy and a market economy has been marked by economic, social and political changes of extraordinary breadth and depth. The talents, skills and knowledge base of the Estonian population are crucial in this process; hence the ambitious scale and urgency of the reforms being advanced for education. Education has been a central priority of the Baltic countries since regaining independence. As a small country with limited natural resources, Estonia sees its human capital as an important asset for entry into the European Union and to compete in the global economy.

This Review offers a comprehensive picture of the significant progress in education reform since Estonia re-established independence. Changes have occurred in the contents of instruction (a new structure and content of curricula), the system of education, institutions (new types of education institutions, a redesigned schooling network) and education provision including new principles of the management and financing of the education system. The OECD examiners whose report forms the basis of this Review, however, concurred with the conclusions of the Government that, despite the progress, the reforms have not resulted from a comprehensive and publicly supported view on the architecture of the Estonian education system and its functioning. Problems have been addressed separately without the necessary co-ordination from the perspective of the whole education system. The Review offers a comprehensive picture of the recently adopted Concept of the Estonian Education System and the Government's Strategy Platform for 2000-2004, which address these problems. The new policy documents provide an overall framework for reform and set forth concrete steps for addressing remaining policy issues at every level of the education system. This Review provides an overview of the impressive forward thinking that has led to these policy statements. Important contributions included "Learning Estonia", developed by the Academic Council convened by the President of the Republic of Estonia, "Estonian Education Strategy" compiled by the Ministry of Education and "Estonian Education Scenarios 2015" designed by the task force of the Committee of the Education Forum. The Review supports these national strategies and offers advice on issues of access, equity, quality, the introduction of new technologies and decentralisation of management and financing responsibilities.

On the basis of background material prepared by the Estonian authorities and information supplied in meetings in the course of site visits, this Review provides an overview of education in the Baltic region and covers the entire system of Estonian education from pre-school through tertiary education and life-long learning for all. The Review gives an analysis of these sectors in light of the economic, social and political context of Estonia. The final chapter, on strategic development, presents a synthesis of the examiners' specific recommendations and sets out how policies can and should be addressed system-wide, linked to priority issues of access and equity, quality, efficiency and governance.

This Review of Education Policy was undertaken within the framework of the Baltic Regional Programme of the OECD Centre for Co-operation with Non-Members (CCNM). Reviews for Latvia and Lithuania are forthcoming as publications in 2001. The conclusions and recommendations of the three country reviews were discussed at a special session of the Education Committee, hosted by Finland on 26 and 27 June 2000 in Helsinki and attended by the Ministers of Education of Estonia, Latvia and Lithuania. This report incorporates key points raised in the course of that discussion.

Members of the review team were: Aims McGuinness (United States), General Rapporteur, Steven Bakker (The Netherlands), Neils Hummeluhr (Denmark), Graham Reid (United Kingdom), Ana-Maria Sandi (The World Bank), Péter Soltész (Hungary), Evelyn Viertel (European Training Foundation) and Ian Whitman (Secretariat).

This volume is published on the responsibility of the Secretary-General of the OECD.

Eric Burgeat
Director
Centre for Co-operation with Non-Members

Table of Contents

Overview of Education Policy Reviews
of Estonia, Latvia and Lithuania

Background of the reviews 9
   Methodology 9
   Importance of the reviews 9
Similarities and differences among Baltic States 11
   Similarities 11
   Differences 13
Phases of Reform 14
Conceptual foundation for reform 15
Common themes 16
   Sector-specific themes 16
   Crosscutting themes 24
Conclusion 27

Chapter 1
Context

Geography 29
History 29
Government 31
Demography 34
Human Resources Index 35
The economy 36
The labour market 39
   Unemployment 39

Chapter 2
Estonian Education System

Legal Famework 45
Policy structure and governance 46
Background of Estonian education system 52
   Early history 52
   Education renewal since 1987 53
Estonian education system 56
Enrolments and student flow 57
Financing 58

Chapter 3

Pre-School and Primary and Secondary
General Education

Description of the system 61
    Legal framework 61
    Pre-school education 61
    Financing 63
    Institutions, enrolments and teachers 64
    Basic and upper secondary general education 66
    Teachers and school directors 68
    Curriculum 73
    Target populations and special needs 79
    School drop-outs 82
Policy Issues and Observations 83
    The evolution of education renewal in Estonia 83
    Curriculum and Assessment 88
    Developing the human resources for education renewal 96
Information and communications technology (ICT) in education 107
Rural schools and the efficiency of the school network 112
Summary of recommendations 117
    National curriculum 117

Chapter 4

Vocational Education and Training

Introduction 123
Description of the system 123
    Legal Framework 123
    Policy structure 125
    Vocational Education and Training System 126
    Institutions and schools/institutional network and study programmes 129
    Financing 137
Issues and observations 138
    Quality and efficiency of the school network 138
    Teachers and teaching 141
    Responsiveness to changing labour market and
    labour market information 143
    Curriculum and Occupational Standards 145
    Examination and certification 146
    Students within the system 147

Adult and continuing education and training 149
Strategy and its implementation 150
Recommendations 152

Chapter 5

Higher Education

Overview of the Estonian higher education system 159
Legal basis 159
Leadership and responsible entities 160
System structure 162
Qualification structure 162
Institutions 165
Quality assurance 167
Language of instruction 170
Financing 170
Science policy and research 171
Issues and Observations 172
Progress in reform 172
Major issues 174
Summary of recommendations 193

Chapter 6

From Forward Thinking to Action

Progress in reform 197
Areas for further improvement 198
Moving from forward-thinking to strategy and action 198
Moving from a system focused on top achievers
to one engaging all learners 199
Aligning national policy and implementation with
the underlying "learner-centred" philosophy of learning Estonia 201
Developing the human resources of the education system 201
Achieving more with the same resources used differently 202
Balancing decentralisation and institutional autonomy
with a new role for MoE 202
Conclusion 203

Selected bibliography 205

Overview of Education Policy Reviews of Estonia, Latvia and Lithuania

This review is one of three of education policy in the Baltic States policy in each of these countries since they regained independence in 1991.

Methodology

The reviews were undertaken by three separate international teams composed of experts and high ranking officials drawn from OECD Member countries and Central and Eastern European States. The same rapporteur, however, participated in each review. Each country provided extensive background data and information. To complement the information gathered for these reviews and to avoid duplication, the OECD reviews drew upon reports of the World Bank, the United Nations Development Programme, the United Nations Children's Fund (UNICEF), the European Training Foundation and other European Union (EU) agencies, and the Soros Foundation as well as other non-governmental organisations. A 1999 OECD review of economic policy in the Baltic States also provided important background information for the education policy reviews.[1]

Importance of the reviews

Education has been a central priority of each of the Baltic States since they regained independence. It is critical to each country's transition from a half-century of Soviet occupation and pervasive impact of Soviet policy, ideology, and command economy. As small countries with limited natural resources, the Baltic States recognise that human capital is among their most important asset to compete in the global economy. All three Baltic States understand that progressive education and training policies are essential pre-requisites to accession to the European Union.

9

The OECD reviews are in-depth analyses of policy affecting all education levels and sectors – from early childhood and pre-school education through the doctoral level. While not a specific subject for review, the teams examined science policy as it interacts with higher education policy. Since education underpins the economic and social well being of all countries, the reviews addressed the links between education and other issues such as the status of women and children, regional economic development, and public administration reform.

The reviews were carried out at the specific request of national authorities. Each government recognised the value of the reviews to contribute to the national debate about the future of education policy and to raise important issues that it would be difficult for authorities within the country to raise.

- The intent of an OECD review is not to evaluate a country's education policy but to place those policies in a comparative perspective. The Baltic States reviews emphasised both themes that cut across all three countries as well as issues that were unique to each country. Particular attention was given to:

- Identifying and respecting the unique geography, demography and economy of each state.

- Identifying good practice in policy and process that could be shared among the three countries and with other OECD Member and Non-Member states.

- Avoiding the uniform application of inappropriate policies to diverse problems.

The reviews focused in particular on the perspective of the state and the public interest and the interaction between state policy and institutions (providers), students/learners, and other clients of the education system (social partners, for example). These relationships are illustrated in Figure 1.

As in countries throughout the world, governments in the Baltic States have been shifting their focus from a primary concern for maintaining and supporting public institutions toward a greater emphasis on encouraging a wider range of providers (*e.g.*, private institutions) to serve student demand and public priorities. The governments are using public policy to ensure responsiveness of the education system to the needs of students/learners and social partners. The OECD teams, therefore, sought to understand how these changes are taking place – and the developing policy issues related to the changes – in each of the Baltic States.

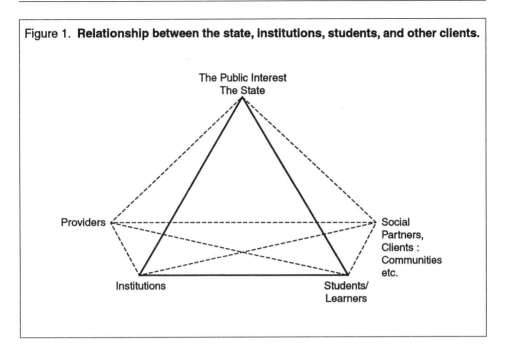

Figure 1. **Relationship between the state, institutions, students, and other clients.**

Similarities and differences among Baltic States

While Estonia, Latvia and Lithuania have a number of points in common, it is important to recognise points of difference that have a direct bearing on education policy.

Similarities

The following is a summary of important similarities:

• Through their early histories, all three countries experienced extended periods of conflict and domination by foreign powers, most notably the Order of Teutonic Knights, Tsarist Russia, German states, and Sweden, and in the case of Lithuania, Poland.

• In the aftermath of World War I, all three countries emerged from more than a century within the Russian Empire to gain independence and membership in the League of Nations. All three countries suffered severely in struggles among German, Russian and other forces in the course of World War I.

- In the initial period of independence, all three countries experienced a period of economic growth, improvement in the standard of living, and development of democratic institutions, although each experienced periods of political instability and threats to democratic institutions.

- All three countries were subjected to the secret conditions of the 1939 Molotov-Ribbentrop Pact between Nazi Germany and the Soviet Union that led to the stationing of Soviet troops and Soviet control in 1940, followed in June 1940 by Nazi invasion and German occupation until the closing months of World War II, when the Soviet Union regained control. During the alternative periods of Soviet and German occupation, hundreds of thousands of Latvians, Lithuanians, and Estonians were either killed or deported to Siberia, and hundreds of thousands of others escaped to other countries.

- All three countries experienced Stalin's brutality as the Soviet Union established control after World War II, including imprisonment and deportation of thousands to Siberia, forced immigration of Russian-speaking populations from the Soviet Union to work on collectivised farms and in large industries, suppression of religion, and imposition of Soviet ideological, military and economic controls.

- In almost 50 years of Soviet occupation, all three countries were subjected to the full force of Soviet ideological, political and economic policies as republics within the Soviet Union. To varying degrees, the Baltic States were afforded limited flexibility to adopt unique education policies reflecting language and culture, but in all other respects the countries were fully integrated into the Soviet Union.

- All three countries experienced a new awakening and drive for independence in the late 1980s in the climate of glasnost and perastroika, and the deterioration of Soviet institutions, culminating in the "Singing Revolution" and the re-establishment of independence in 1990 and 1991. (Lithuania re-established independence on March 11, 1990, Estonia on August 20, 1991, and Latvia on August 21, 1991.

- Upon re-establishing independence, all three countries reverted to Constitutions based largely upon those established in the initial period of independence after World War I.

- All three countries have moved aggressively to adopt progressive governmental, economic, social, and education reforms. All three countries have been accepted as candidates for accession to the European Union.

Differences

Several significant differences among the Baltic States, however, are especially important to an understanding of differences in education policy:

- All three countries had unique early histories and relations with other nations and cultures that have had lasting effects on culture and language and continue to influence national perspectives and policy. Lithuania has at times been linked to – and often has had contentious relations with – Poland over its history (Vilnius was part of Poland until World War II). Large parts of Estonia and Latvia were the country of Livonia until the mid-XVIth century. Latvia and Estonia have historically had closer ties with the Nordic countries than Lithuania – Estonia with Finland, Denmark and Sweden, and Latvia with Denmark and Sweden.

- Estonian, Latvian and Lithuanian are three highly distinct languages. Latvian and Lithuanian belong to the Baltic-branch of the Indo-European language family. Estonian belongs to the Finno-Ugric family of languages – along with Finnish, Hungarian, Udmurt, Sami, Komi, Mari, Livonian, and Mordvinian.

- Lithuania is a more ethnically homogeneous country than Estonia and Latvia. In 1999, Lithuanians comprised 81.3% of the populations, and Russians (8.4%) and Poles (7%) constituted the largest minority populations. In contrast, 55.7% of Latvia's population was Latvian and 32.2% were ethnic Russians. In Estonia, 65.2% were Estonians and 28.1% were ethnic Russians. The high percentage of ethnic Russians – especially in Estonia and Latvia – reflects the years of forced immigration, especially in the post-World War II period. Since re-establishment of independence, all three countries have experienced an out-migration of Russian populations, although out-migration has slowed considerably in recent years. Within Latvia and Estonia, the concentrations of ethnic Russian population tend to be in the major urban areas (Riga and Tallinn), and in regions associated with former Soviet industries or large collective farms.

- In Estonia and Latvia the largest religious group is Lutheran but in Lithuania it is Roman Catholic.

- All three countries are parliamentary republics in which the Government is headed by a Prime Minister appointed by the president, and a council (Latvia and Estonia) or cabinet (Latvia) of ministers, and a president who is head of state. In contrast to Estonia and Latvia where the president is elected by the parliament and plays a largely ceremonial role, the President of Lithuania is elected by popular election to a five-year term and has broader executive powers than the presidents of the other two countries.

- All three countries have pursued economic reforms to move dramatically from the command economy totally controlled by and oriented toward the Soviet Union, to market economies with increasingly strong relationships with Europe and the global economy. Each, however, has pursued independent economic policies with consequent differences in key economic indicators.[2]

Phases of Reform

Education reform in the Baltic States is best understood in terms of phases beginning in the late 1980s. Each country's reforms can be traced to initiatives in 1988 (if not earlier) undertaken in the spirit of the new awakening, perestroika, and the deterioration of Soviet institutions. In this period, each country experienced unprecedented grass roots engagement of educators in the exploration of new possibilities – initially within the Soviet Union, and then increasingly with the realisation that full re-establishment of independence was possible.

In the 1990-1992 period all three countries re-established independence and established Constitutions (based largely on earlier Constitutions) and the initial legal framework for education. Each country enacted a basic framework law, a Law on Education, for the education system. While each of these initial education laws reflects unique points for each country, the laws include common points regarding democratic principles, freedom from the ideological controls of the past, opportunities for private institutions, and significantly increased autonomy for universities. Enacted in the rapidly developing circumstances of 1991, these initial laws would require further refinement in later years.

In the 1992-1994 period, each of the Baltic States faced extraordinary challenges in gaining economic stability and establishing new legal frameworks and institutional structures. The economic dislocation in the collapse of the Soviet-oriented command economy and the slow development of new social and economic policies created severe hardships for each country's education systems. Nevertheless, each country continued to make progress on basic elements of education reform: eliminating ideologically oriented elements within universities, development of new curricula, textbooks, and teaching materials, and developing new links with Western donors and partners such as the Soros Foundation, the British Council, and the European Union Phare programme.

The 1995-1996 period brought a temporary pause in the positive developments since re-establishing independence as banking crises and economic instability drew attention and energy away from education reform. This was also a period in which the governments in each country attempted to shape new state policies to provide a degree of order and direction (*e.g.*, through national curricula and standards) to the previously largely decentralised and often fragmented reforms.

In the 1996-1998 period, all three countries experienced their strongest periods of economic revitalisation and growth since 1991. In education reform, each country broadened the conceptual foundation for education reform and developed the second generation of legal frameworks for general education, vocational and professional education, and higher education. The Laws on Education first enacted in 1991-1992 were either replaced or amended significantly to reflect an increased maturity in each country's education reforms. Each country embarked on the development of new national curricula and assessment/testing policies, drawing on the expertise of foreign advisors and reflecting the best practice of many Western countries.

The Russian economic crisis beginning with the devaluation of the rouble on August 17th, 1998 slowed the economic growth as well as the pace of education reform of the previous two years in all three countries. This pause was clearly evident at the time of the site visits for the OECD reviews in 1999. Yet the commitment to reform remained strong as evidenced by continued progress on national curricula, new assessment policies, development of new textbooks and teaching materials, and enactment of new laws for non-university higher education ("colleges"). The countries continued to make progress on higher education reform through continued strengthening of the capacity of universities to accommodate escalating demand and the international expectations for quality in academic programmes and research.

Conceptual foundation for reform

As mentioned above, all three countries adopted framework Laws on Education in 1991 (Lithuania and Latvia) and 1992 (Estonia) that included similar concepts and principles. At the same time, each country pursued a different path in the development of a conceptual foundation for education reform.

Lithuania provides the clearest example of the development of a basic document, the 1992 General Concept of Education in Lithuania, which has served as the foundation of education reform and legislation throughout the pre- and post-independence periods. The Concept sets out four phases: phase I from-the end of 1988 to March 11, 1990; phase II leading to the framing of the Concept in 1992; and phases III and IV (1992 to 2005) during which "a uniform, permanent Lithuanian educational system is created covering formal and informal education and an expanded network of public and private educational institutions."

In both Estonia and Latvia, the development of a broadly accepted conceptual foundation for education reform has been more of an evolving process. In Estonia, for example, not until the late 1990s did a broad consensus emerge around the concept "Learning Estonia", developed by the Academic Council convened by the President of the Republic of Estonia, "Estonian Education Strategy" compiled by the Ministry of Education and "Estonian Education Scenarios 2015" designed by the task force of the Committee of the Education Forum. In Latvia, the Ministry of Education and Science developed a "Latvian Concept of Education" in 1995, but from the observations of the OECD team, this document did not receive wide acceptance as the foundation for reform. Nevertheless, despite changes in governments, Latvian education reform has evolved on the basis of an informal consensus about the principles that should guide the country's education system.

In their reports, the OECD review teams emphasised the importance of a broad understanding of and commitment to the principles of education reform as an essential condition for sustained progress and for translating concepts into strategies and actions – especially in the case of frequent changes in political leadership. Such an understanding and commitment must reach not only to all levels of the education system but also to the nation's political and civic leadership and social partners. Whether or not the conceptual foundation is reflected in a formal document, all three countries face the challenge of engaging the society as a whole in the process of change.

Common themes

Despite the clear differences among Estonia, Latvia, and Lithuania, the OECD teams observed a number of common themes in education policy shared by all three countries. These can be divided between sector-specific themes and those that cut across all sectors.

Sector-specific themes

All three countries are engaged in reform of each level and sector of their education systems from pre-school through higher education. The issues identified by the OECD teams most often related to the points of inter-section or transition. Examples include:

- The inter-section between education and broader social and economic problems such as the relationship of pre-school education to the health and welfare of young children and women, and the relationship of vocational education to the changing economy and labour market.

- The transition between pre-school education and compulsory education and policies to ensure that all young children are prepared and ready to learn.

- The transition between compulsory education and upper-secondary education and policies designed to ensure that a wider range of students complete compulsory education with the depth and breadth of academic preparation to pursue further education or to enter the labour market – and to continue learning throughout their lifetimes.

- The transition between upper-secondary general and professional/vocational education (grades 10 through 12) and either the labour market or higher education.

The following are highlights of the themes related to the major sectors.

Strengthening Pre-school/ Early Childhood Education

In all three countries, pre-school enrolment dropped precipitously following independence as the countries moved away from the extensive network of preschool establishments linked to Soviet-era working places. The need to ensure that all young children are prepared for compulsory education is a shared concern, but the approaches being taken to address the issues differ. At the time of the OECD review, Lithuania was moving to lower the age of the beginning of compulsory education from age 7 to include children in "zero" level classes (generally 6-year olds). Latvia extended compulsory education to include pre-school education in the Law on Education enacted in 1998 but repealed this provision (primarily for economic reasons) in 1999. Estonia is taking steps to strengthen pre-school education including strengthening the requirements for teacher preparation and establishing new financing policies. The OECD reviews strongly supported the initiatives to achieve the goal of ensuring that all young children are prepared to enter school, but the teams raised concerns about the adequacy of resources, training of teachers and other support – especially in rural areas – to make this goal a reality. Another common concern is that there should be strong links between state initiatives aimed at improving the health and welfare of young children and women and policies related to pre-school education. In some cases, the responsibility for these inter-related areas is divided among different ministries.

Strengthening (extending) compulsory education and improving the quality of education for all students

Reform of compulsory education has been a central focus of education reform in all three Baltic States since the late 1980s. All countries moved rapidly to "de-ideologise" the curriculum and to establish the basis and transition process (curriculum, textbooks, and curricular materials, and retraining of teachers) for education systems in which the language of instruction was primarily in the national language (Estonian, Latvian, or Lithuanian). In the initial years, reform was largely a grass-roots phenomenon with great variation throughout the countries in the extent and direction of change. Multiple well-intentioned but often unco-ordinated foreign initiatives and pilots both stimulated reform and contributed indirectly to the lack of coherence in education reform. By the mid-1990s, however, each country moved to develop national curricula and standards and began the process of developing quality assurance mechanisms such as centrally set and/or administered assessments and examinations. The countries faced – and continue to face – a number of common problems:

- Refining the initial assessment and testing instruments to ensure that they reflect the goals of national curricula such as integration of knowledge and practice and active learning.

- Narrowing the gap between the goals of reform and the realities of change at the classroom and school levels including the need for basic instructional materials, teacher in-service education, and other support.

- Increasing the coherence in the often-fragmented provision of teacher in-service education and a stronger link of the available programmes to implementation of new curriculum and assessment policies.

- Undertaking fundamental reform of pre-service teacher education to reflect the principles of education reform.

- Ensuring quality across diverse systems.

- Addressing the problems of small rural schools and severe differences between urban and rural areas in the quality and cost-effectiveness of schools.

With the assistance of the Soros Foundation and Phare and other external assistance, the Baltic States have made impressive progress in extending the application of information technology (ICT), especially access to computers and the Internet, throughout their education systems, but especially in compulsory/general education. Estonia's Tiger Leap initiative, for example, which began as a commitment to ensure that all students had access to computers, has evolved into a far broader initiative aimed at ensuring that Estonians are prepared to thrive and compete in the global information economy.

Reforming post-compulsory education (upper secondary education)

Many of the issues that relate to compulsory education (*e.g.* curriculum, standards, quality assurance, and teacher training) were also evident at the post-compulsory (upper-secondary) level. A basic challenge faced by all three countries is to provide a larger proportion of each post-compulsory age cohort with a broader general education within either general secondary education schools (gymnasiums) or secondary vocational education. In Soviet times, many academically weaker students entered vocational schools directly following compulsory education to be trained for narrowly defined working places in state-owned enterprises. Only limited general education was included in that training. Other students entered secondary vocational schools to prepare for specialised technical fields that required a broader general education foundation but generally did not prepare students further education at the university level, although some students continued in specialised post-secondary education training.

With the collapse of the command economy linked to the Soviet Union, the state enterprises for which vocational schools trained students ceased to exist. A combination of low-prestige and outdated training programmes, equipment and teachers contributed to a precipitous decline in demand for secondary vocational education.

The pattern in the post-independence period in all three Baltic countries has been to lengthen the period of general education for all students and to delay specialisation. An increasing proportion of those completing compulsory education is seeking to enter general secondary education – and, if possible, more highly selective gymnasiums – which will increase the chances for university entrance. At the same time, vocational secondary education is converging with general secondary education, as countries are developing new national standards and examinations for grade 12 that all students much complete – whether in general or vocational secondary education. The increased demand for vocational education is at the post-secondary level for students who have completed secondary education and seek specialised training to enter the labour market.

Common developments across the three countries include:

• Continuing development of national curricula and standards;

• Implementation of externally developed and administered grade 12 examinations;

• Gaining acceptance of universities of the use of grade 12 examinations for university entrance (this is in place in Estonia and under consideration in Lithuania and Latvia);

• Diversifying upper secondary education through "profiling" (Lithuania) and other changes in the curriculum to accommodate a wider range of student abilities and aspirations.

Reforming vocational education and training

As described above, the vocational education and training systems of all three countries were closely tied to the Soviet command economy. Outdated curricula, obsolete equipment and training materials, deteriorating facilities, and teachers who were ill-prepared for new professions and market economy combined to make the vocational education and training systems largely irrelevant to the developing labour market.

All three Baltic countries have made important progress in reform of vocational education and training over the decade of the 1990s – stimulated by the goal of EU accession and supported by foreign assistance. The EU Phare programme and the European Training Foundation (ETF) have played significant, positive roles in developing conceptual and strategic basis for reform, and in supporting pilot programmes in areas such as curriculum development, regional training and development, and teacher training. In the 1997-99 period, all three countries completed work on and enacted new framework laws on vocational education and training. These new laws establish national qualification systems, provide for extensive involvement of social partners at every level, clarify the roles of different schools, establish new non-university sectors (ISCED 4B and 5B), and strengthen the links between vocational education and training and regional economic development. Common issues faced by all three countries included:

• Moving from concepts and strategies to concrete actions. While the basic legal framework and formal policy structures are in place, all three countries need to accelerate implementation of concrete reforms. Foreign assistance has been an indispensable catalyst for reform, but implementing and sustaining reform will require stronger leadership and funding from the countries themselves.

- Establishing state leadership structures for co-ordination of vocational education and training across all ministries. Estonia and Lithuania have recently transferred responsibility for agricultural vocational education and training institutions from the Ministry of Agriculture to the Ministry of Education with the result most vocational training institutions are now under a single ministry. In Latvia, responsibility for these institutions continues to be shared by several ministries, although the Ministry of Education and Science has overall co-ordinating responsibility. Developing effective co-ordination between the state vocational education system and state employment services – the entity responsible for labour market information, short-term training of the unemployed, and regional labour market services under the jurisdiction of another ministry – remains an issue in all three countries.

- Optimising the school network. All three countries face the problem of two many small, highly specialised vocational schools. Each is taking actions to close or merge schools and to modernise and broaden the profiles of other schools. In some instances, secondary vocational schools, or technicums, are evolving into "colleges" at the ISCED 4B level and being linked with other institutions to form complexes that are more cost-effective.

- Clarifying the roles of the developing "colleges". The development of post-secondary institutions at the non-university level is evolving in each of the countries, yet there remains a degree of ambiguity about the role and mission of these new institutions. All the vocational education and training reforms have emphasised the need for a new sector at the non-university level to train highly skilled technicians for the developing labour market. All the reforms emphasise that these institutions should relate "horizontally" to the labour market and should be closely linked with social partners. When fully developed, such institutions should also provide an alternative to university-level education. Essentially two kinds of institutions are developing. First, institutions at the post-secondary level evolving from former "technicums" but not oriented toward preparation for university entrance (ISCED 1997 4B); and second, colleges offering university-level professional programmes (ISCED 1997 5B) that are more clearly linked to universities and, in some cases, are governed by universities. In part because the demand in the labour market for specialists trained at the ISCED 4B and 5B levels is still developing, many of the students attending these institutions still aspire primarily to pursue a university education rather than enter the labour market following training. The potential proliferation of new post-secondary or higher education institutions raises fundamental policy questions about quality assurance and financing for all three countries.

- Engaging social partners. The development of stronger roles for social partners in the reform of vocational education and training is a clear need in all three countries. Participation of social partners is needed in the new national qualification systems, advising in the design of training programmes, providing apprenticeship and other work-site training, and providing up-to-date equipment and training materials.

- Training of vocational education teachers. The retraining of current teachers and training of new teachers is a major need throughout the Baltic States.

Reforming tertiary education

All three Baltic States have made great strides in restructuring their higher education system since the major changes began in 1988. Changes included:

- Instilling democratic principles and processes throughout the universities.

- Establishing a new legal framework providing for institutions of higher education, university autonomy, a new research infrastructure, the framework for quality assurance, and a differentiated higher education-system.

- Eliminating previous restrictions in content and pedagogy, especially in the social sciences and humanities, and eliminating required military retraining as a compulsory part of the curriculum.

- Carrying out dramatic shifts in academic programmes in response to changing student demands and the economic reality of the need to generate additional revenue from fee-paying students to offset limitations in state funding.

- Moving from the narrow Soviet degree structure to an award structure that is not only more flexible but also consistent with Western models and increasing expectations (*e.g.*, Bologna) for common structures across Europe and the world.

- Abolishing the academies of science as research organisations, reconstituting the academies as honorary societies, and integrating research into the universities, resulting in substantial gains in research and greatly strengthened universities.

- Strengthening graduate education, especially through the integration of research and teaching at the doctoral level in contrast to the location of doctoral programmes outside the universities in Soviet times.

At the time of the OECD reviews, there was growing recognition that further changes in higher education policies would be necessary. In Lithuania, for example, a new Law on Institutions of Higher Education in Lithuania was under consideration. Major issues remaining at the time of the reviews included:

- Accommodating the escalating demand for university-level education, including alternatives such as non-university "colleges."

- Tightening quality assurance requirements, including stronger requirements for non-public institutions.

- Reforming the financing of higher education, including the highly sensitive issue of student fees.

- Conforming degree structures to international expectations as defined by the Bologna Joint Declaration.

- Developing new modes of delivery including open-distance learning and greatly expanded use of information technology throughout the higher education system.

- Seeking solutions, including strengthened doctoral programmes and international affiliations, to the problem of retraining current professors and developing the next generation of faculty and researchers.

- Reforming university programmes for teacher education.

Having granted universities substantial autonomy at the time of re-establishing independence, all three countries are now debating ways to increase the responsiveness of higher education institutions to public priorities and to ensure greater public accountability. At the time of the OECD reviews, each country was debating measures that would provide for a stronger role for the

State in setting priorities while enhancing the quality, responsiveness and international competitiveness of the universities and other higher education institutions.

Strengthening adult education and lifelong learning

The Baltic states face a common need to prepare their adult populations to participate in democratic society and a market economy, and to continue to learn and adjust to the dramatic changes occurring in the technology-intensive global economy. Nevertheless, the institutional network remains largely oriented to students who have recently completed compulsory or upper secondary education and is not effectively linked or co-ordinated with the labour market training network.

All three countries have expressed policy commitments to lifelong learning and established new legal frameworks for adult education, but a major challenge remains to translate these policies into concrete implementation. New developments in the use of information technology and open-distance learning (open universities) show promise as means to provide access for the adult population to further education and training. As the economies develop, employers should play an increasing role in the demand for accessible training opportunities. Other providers – primarily non-public institutions – are responding to the need, but these programmes tend to be in areas where the demand and potential for economic gain are greatest (business, law, and foreign languages) and are available primarily in the urban areas. State policies for regulating quality continue to be weak and the cost of non-public programmes makes them inaccessible to large segments of the adult population.

Crosscutting themes

As reflected in the summary of sector-specific themes, the OECD teams identified a number of crosscutting themes that are evident in all three Baltic States.

Strengthening and sustaining national policy leadership for education reform

Frequent changes in governments and ministers of education have created serious problems for all three Baltic States in sustaining national policy leadership for education reform. In face of this instability, the countries have benefited from a general consensus within education networks and among major political parties and non-governmental organisations (NGOs) about the conceptual foundations and goals of education reform. External forces, such as the expectations established for accession to the EU, have played a key role in sustaining reform. Within the constraints of leadership changes, limited resources, and under-developed civil service laws, all three countries have made progress in reforming the roles and functioning of the ministries of education. Common goals of these reforms include:

- Shifting the oversight and quality assurance emphasis from controlling and inspecting "inputs" (e.g., detailed curriculum and curriculum timetables), toward overseeing the accomplishment of "outcomes" while allowing schools and institutions greater independence in shaping the details of implementation.

- Strengthening the professional qualifications of ministry personnel.

- Emphasising decentralisation and deregulation.

- Strengthening the ministry capacity for strategic planning and policy leadership.

- Increasing the co-ordination between government initiatives and initiatives supported by NGOs and foreign sponsors.

- Despite these promising developments, the OECD teams observed that all three countries face a challenge in broadening and deepening the commitment of society – especially political leaders and social partners p– to education reform as a fundamental foundation for essentially all the countries' major policy goals. The countries also all face the challenge of sustaining attention to education reform across the inevitable changes in government. The specific mechanism for addressing these challenges will be different in each country, but the leadership must come from the highest levels of government and will likely require extensive use of non-governmental organisations that can provide for continuity when government cannot do so.

As mentioned at several points in this overview, EU Phare, the Soros Foundation, and other foreign sponsors have provided invaluable stimulus and support for education reform in all three Baltic States. Foreign assistance is not a satisfactory long-term substitute for permanent, sustained leadership within each country. The OECD teams were concerned that, as foreign-supported pilot projects and NGOs phase out their support in critical areas such as reform of vocational education and training, the commitment and capacity to sustain reform may not exist.

*Narrowing the gap between concepts/strategies and the realities of practice
and implementation*

All three countries have developed essential legal and policy frameworks. However, in large part because of the instability in national leadership, the countries face significant problems in moving to practical application. This is especially evident in the general secondary and vocational education and training systems in which a significant gap remains between the reform goals and the realities of change at the level of the school and classroom. The national leaders expressed concern about this gap in the course of the OECD reviews and all three countries will be giving more attention to the basic infrastructure and support systems necessary to deepen the impact of reform. Greater emphasis on alignment of teacher pre-service and in-service education and training of school directors with reform goals are examples of such efforts. As mentioned above, developing the commitment and capacity to assume responsibility and sustain initiatives originated through foreign sponsors will be especially important in bridging the gap between strategy and practice.

Addressing concerns about equity and fairness

All three Baltic States have made strong commitments to civil liberties and to narrowing the gaps in access and opportunity for all people within their countries. They recognise that fulfilling these commitments is an essential condition for modern democracies, for accession to the European Union, and for full participation in the global economy. In the OECD education policy reviews, the teams underscored the need for further progress on:

- Narrowing the disparities in quality and educational opportunity between urban and rural areas (including the need for public administration reform to address the problems of small municipalities that lack the capacity to sustain strong schools).

- Ensuring that special needs students are served, including addressing the health and economic needs of young children to ensure that they are ready to learn.

- Continuing to make progress on addressing the needs of language and ethnic minority populations to ensure that they can be full participants in the civic and economic life of the countries.

- Countering the strong tendencies toward elite secondary schools and a focus on university entrance with deliberate steps to ensure that all students – not only the most academically gifted and those with social and economic advantages – have access to quality education and the opportunity to gain essential knowledge and skills.

Recognising the impact of government reform on education policy

In the course of the education policy reviews, the OECD teams were repeatedly reminded that the progress of education reform often depends on reform of other areas of government. As examples:

- Resolution of questions of public administration reform will have a direct impact on the progress of education reform. While the specific legal and financial responsibilities of municipalities for education differ among the three countries, each faces the problem of small rural municipalities that lack the capacity to fulfil their education responsibilities. Each of the Baltic States faces fundamental issues related to the structure, roles, and financing of municipal governments and about appropriate roles and responsibilities of entities between municipalities and the national government (regions, counties, or other entities).

- Reforming civil services policies. Civil service reform across all levels of government is a critical prerequisite for strengthening the policy leadership, analytic, oversight, and support functions of ministries of education and other governmental units responsible for education.

- Aligning state finance policies with education reform. In each of the Baltic States, the ministry of finance plays a critical and often dominant role in education policy, yet, from the observations of the OECD review teams, these policies are not always consistent with or supportive of education reform goals. The issues are not only on the level of state financing of education, but also on the details of policy implementation. As emphasised earlier, continued progress in education reform will require leadership and co-ordination at the highest level of government and across all ministries with responsibilities that have an impact on education.

Conclusion

The human resources of Estonia, Latvia and Lithuania are these countries' most valuable assets. As small countries with comparatively limited natural resources, the Baltic States' future will depend on the knowledge and skills of their people. Education of all the people, not only young children and youth but also adults, should be each nation's highest priority.

The Baltic States have made extraordinary progress in education reform over the past decade. The OECD teams were especially impressed by the dedication of teachers, professors, school directors and university leaders who, despite exceptionally difficult times, have persevered, maintained quality, and led the way in changes necessary to prepare students for participation in democracy and a market economy. The OECD teams are confident that the leaders in each of the countries have the vision and commitment to ensure continued progress in education reform into the XXIst century.

Notes

1. , OECD Economic Surveys: The Baltic States, A Regional Economic Assessment. Paris: OECD, 2000.

2. See OECD, The Baltic States, A Regional Economic Assessment.

Chapter 1

Context

Geography

The Republic of Estonia (Eesti Vabariik) lies on the eastern shores of the Baltic Sea and covers 45 227 square kilometres. The country is situated on the level of the northwest part of the East European platform, on which there are only slight variations in elevation. The highest point (Suur Munamägi) is 318 metres above sea level. Estonia has over 1 500 islands and more than 1 400 lakes. Natural resources include shale oil (kukersite), peat, phosphorite, amber, Cambrian blue clay, limestone, and dolomite. Land use includes 25% arable land, 11% permanent pastures, 44% forests and woodland and 20% other uses.

History

For centuries, the area that is now the Republic of Estonia was repeatedly contested in battles involving local tribes, Russians, German knights, Denmark, Sweden, Poland and Lithuania. The Estonian language first appeared in print in 1525. In the XVIIth century, the Swedish period in Estonian history was marked by cultural advancement. Tartu University opened in 1632 and by the close of the century nearly every parish had a school. Russia gained control of Estonia in 1710, and in the subsequent 200 years of tsarist rule, Estonia's peasants lived in the same conditions of near-slavery as the serfs of Russia.

Literacy began to spread in the XIXth century and Estonian-language periodicals and literature appeared. Between 1856 and 1863 Tsar Alexander II gradually granted Estonian serfs rights to education, land ownership and free movement within and outside the territory. The National Awakening marked thesecond half of the XIXth century. The song festival, held in Tartu in 1869, represented the first public demonstration of Estonian national identity. However, Tsar Alexander III stifled this awakening when he came to power in 1881, initiating a period of intense Russification.

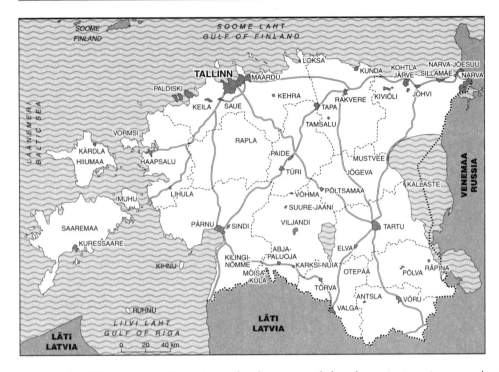

In the XXth century, Estonia took advantage of the chaos in Russia caused by World War I and the Bolshevik Revolution, declaring independence on February 24, 1918. But by the end of February, Germany had taken the infant country by force. When Germany capitulated in November 1918, the Red forces moved in. The War for Independence lasted 13 months ending in the Tartu Peace Treaty, signed February 2, 1920, in which the Soviet Russia renounced claims to the territory "for all time". In 1921 the Republic of Estonia was accepted into the League of Nations and reforms progressed quickly and social welfare laws were established on a par with those in Europe.

A political crisis in the mid-1930s brought Estonia to the verge of authoritarianism. President Konstantin Päts banned political parties and restricted civil rights but maintained popular support. On August 23, 1939, the USSR and Germany secretly signed the Molotov-Ribbentrop pact, carving Eastern Europe into spheres of influence and the Baltic States fell to the USSR. On June 16, Soviet troops began occupying Estonia and Estonia was officially taken over by the USSR. In all, within 12 months of Soviet rule in 1940-41, 59 700 people disappeared in Estonia, of whom around 1 000 were executed. By the end of 1941, the Nazis gained control of Estonia from the Soviets and maintained occupation for three years. After intense battles, the Soviets regained control in March 1944.

In the first years of the renewed Soviet regime, 36 000 Estonians were arrested and accused of aiding the Nazis. At the same time 30 000 to 35 000 people fled to the woods to organise resistance that continued into the 1950s. During the German and Soviet occupations and the War for Independence, Estonia lost approximately 200 000 people. But despite these losses the Estonian national identity survived 50 years of Soviet occupation.

From the mid-1970s and through the 1980s, Estonians protested against Soviet control and demands for restoration of independence intensified. A new National Awakening began in 1987, as protests against the system became more frequent and open. On February 24 1988, 3 000 Estonians demonstrated on the anniversary of the first Estonian Republic, and then in October and November, more than 860 000 people signed a petition protesting amendments to the USSR constitution that would have increased centralised power. On November 16, the Supreme Soviet of the Estonian SSR passed a declaration of sovereignty.

In March 1990, the Estonian Communist Party declared independence from the central party, and in May, the Estonian Soviet Socialist Republic was officially renamed the Republic of Estonia. In 1991, a rapid succession of dramatic events culminated in re-establishment of independence and the collapse of the Soviet Union. On March 3, 1991, 78% of voters cast their vote for independence in a referendum. During the failed Moscow coup, military units landed in Estonia and blockaded the harbour. Estonia declared independence on August 20 and the USSR recognised Estonian independence on August 24, the United States renewed diplomatic ties on September 2, the United Nations accepted the Baltic States on September 17, and finally, the USSR ceased to exist on December 21.

In the period since independence was re-established, Estonia has made steady progress toward the goal of accession to the European Union. In 1993, Estonia was accepted as a full member of the Council of Europe and in 1995, the Free Trade agreement with the EU went into effect. Also, Estonia signed an Association Agreement with the EU, and submitted a formal application for EU membership. In 1997, Estonia was invited to begin EU accession negotiations in April 1998.[1]

Government

The Constitution approved by referendum on June 28, 1992 establishes the principles of the rule of law. It recognises the principle of separate and balanced courts, guarantees of fundamental human rights and liberties according to universally recognised principles and norms. Estonia is a democratic parliamentary republic wherein the supreme power is vested in the people. Citizens exercise this power by electing the Riigikogu (parliament) and by participating in referendums. The Riigikogu has 101 members elected by popular vote to serve four-year terms. The last election was held in March 1999.

Executive power rests with the Government headed by the Prime Minister. The cabinet is the Council of Ministers appointed by the Prime Minister and approved by Parliament. The head of State of Estonia is the President of the Republican, the judicial branch is the National Court of which the Riigikogu appoints the chairman.

Estonia has 15 counties (maakonnad, singular – maakond), 43 towns and 204 rural municipalities. The Constitution establishes two levels of government: the state and municipalities. County governments are units of and have powers delegated from the State. Counties (the major town in the county is in parentheses) include Harjumaa (Tallinn), Hiiumaa (Kardla), Ida-Virumaa (Johvi), Jarvamaa (Paide), Jogevamaa (Jogeva), Laanemaa (Haapsalu), Laane-Virumaa (Rakvere), Parnumaa (Parnu), Polvamaa (Polva), Raplamaa (Rapla), Saaremaa (Kuessaare), Tartumaa (Tartu), Valgamaa (Valga), Viljandimaa (Viljandi), Vorumaa (Voru).

Table 1. **Resident population as of January 1, 1989 to 2000**

Year	Resident population at the beginning of year	Per cent change from previous year
1989	1565.7	
1991	1570.5	
1992	1562.2	0.5%
1993	1526.5	2.3%
1994	1506.9	1.3%
1995	1491.6	1.0%
1996	1476.3	1.0%
1997	1462.1	1.0%
1998	1453.8	0.6%
1999	1445.6	0.6%
2000	1439.2	0.4%

Source: Statistical Office of Estonia, June 2000.

Table 2. **Demographic characteristics, 1989 to 1999**

	1989	1991	1992	1993	1994	1995	1996	1997	1998	1999
Births per 1000 population	11.81	12.5 8	13.02	14.02	14.77	14. 07	12.95	12.73	13.41	
Live births		19.3	18.0	15.3	14.1	13.6	13.3	12.6	12.3	
Death cases		19.7	20.1	21.2	21.8	20.9	19.0	18.6	19.4	
Natural increase		- 0.4	- 2.1	- 6.1	- 8.0	- 7.3	- 5.7	- 6.0	- 7.2	
Net Migration		- 8.0	- 33.8	- 13.8	- 7.6	- 8.2	- 5.7	- 2.5	- 1.1	
Urban		1 121.0	1 112.9	1 077.4	1 058.8	1 044.2	1 030.0	1 021.2		
Rural		449.4	449.3	449.1	448.1	447.4	4 46.3	440.9		
Males									676 635.0	672 676.0
Females									777 209.0	772 904.0
Estonians	963.3				962.3	957.9	953.5	950.1	946.6	942.5
Russians	474.8				436.6	428.4	420.4	412.6	409.1	406.0
Ukrainians	48.3				40.5	39.6	38.6	37.3	36.9	36.7
Other nationalities	79.3				67.5	65.7	63.8	62.1	61.2	60.4

Source: Statistical Office of Estonia, June 2000.

Demography

The estimated population of Estonia as of January 1, 2000 was 1 437 197, a decrease of 0.4% from the previous January. From 1991 to 2000, the population decreased 8.4% (from 1 570 451 to 1 439 197).

The most precipitous decline occurred directly following restoration of independence between 1992 and 1993 when the population decreased 2.3% primarily as a result of emigration of the ethnic Russian population. Net migration decreased from a high of 33 827 in 1992 to 1 131 in 1998. The ethnic Russian population decreased 8% from 1989 to 1994, and 7% from 1994 to 1999. By 1999, the ethnic composition of the population was Estonian 65.2%, Russian 28.1%, Ukrainian 2.5%, and Finnish .9%.

Of more significance for the education and training system is a fall in the number of births. The birth rate has been declining steadily over the past decade. The number of live births per year decreased from 19 320 in 1991 to 12 269 in 1998 and the number of live births per 100 population decreased from 14.2 to

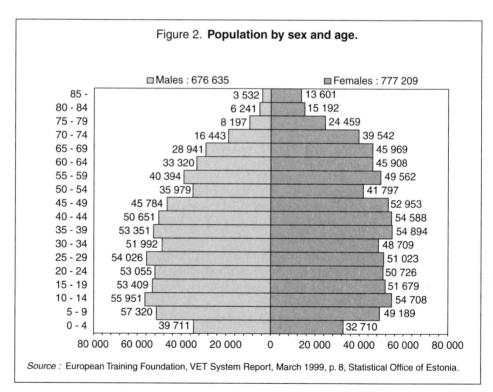

Figure 2. **Population by sex and age.**

□ Males : 676 635   ■ Females : 777 209

Age	Males	Females
85 -	3 532	13 601
80 - 84	6 241	15 192
75 - 79	8 197	24 459
70 - 74	16 443	39 542
65 - 69	28 941	45 969
60 - 64	33 320	45 908
55 - 59	40 394	49 562
50 - 54	35 979	41 797
45 - 49	45 784	52 953
40 - 44	50 651	54 588
35 - 39	53 351	54 894
30 - 34	51 992	48 709
25 - 29	54 026	51 023
20 - 24	53 055	50 726
15 - 19	53 409	51 679
10 - 14	55 951	54 708
5 - 9	57 320	49 189
0 - 4	39 711	32 710

80 000   60 000   40 000   20 000   0   20 000   40 000   60 000   80 000

Source : European Training Foundation, VET System Report, March 1999, p. 8, Statistical Office of Estonia.

8.46 in the same period. The falling numbers joining the education system, and the reduction over the years in the total number of pupils, will have wide effects, initially on primary schools but in due course on all parts of the system. Among the issues which will arise are the required number of teachers at various stages, the number of schools, the viability of small schools in rural areas, and the scale and composition of vocational and higher education. Most importantly, the system must be able to adjust to new circumstances and this will necessitate a high degree of flexibility and innovation.

One-third of the population is under age 25, and 14.3% is 65 or older (see Figure 2). Women constitute 53% of the population, a percentage that has remained approximately the same since the restoration of independence. Reflecting the lower life expectancy for men, women constitute a higher proportion of the population in the older age groups.[2]

Human Resources Index

Estonia had a Human Development Index (HDI) of 0.773 in 1999 as shown in Table 3. The 1999 Human Development Report points out that the economy (GNP Index) is the major element of the index that must improve if Estonia is to improve its overall ranking. The current ranking is at a medium level compared to other countries. Because of the slowed rate of increase in GDP in 1998 and

Table 3. **Human development index component indices in the Baltic and Nordic countries, 1999 report according to 1997 statistical indicators**

	Life Expectancy Index	Education Index	GDP Index	HDI
Estonia	0.73	0.93	0.66	0.773
Lithuania	0.75	0.91	0.62	0.761
Latvia	0.72	0.90	0.61	0.744
Iceland	0.90	0.95	0.90	0.919
Norway	0.89	0.98	0.92	0.927
Sweden	0.89	0.99	0.88	0.923
Finland	0.86	0.99	0.89	0.913
Denmark	0.84	0.96	0.91	0.905

Source: United Nations Development Program, "Estonia's opportunities and human development rankings," Estonian Human Development Report 1999, Tallinn: UNDP, 1999, p. 12.

1999 (see below), a rapid improvement in the ranking seems unlikely in the near future.[3]

The economy

Like all other countries of the former Soviet Union, Estonia faced major problems of economic adjustment when it regained independence in 1991. Indeed the difficulties for Estonia (and the other Baltic countries) were considerably greater than for the countries of Central and Eastern Europe. Estonia is very small and its economy has traditionally been very closely integrated with that of the Soviet Union. It was a producer of goods on a far larger scale than would have been warranted by the domestic economy, and many of its enterprises were based on production using raw materials imported from the Soviet Union with the final output then being exported to that country. The agricultural sector was based on large-scale production, on collective farms, on meat and milk production for Soviet markets. In addition, Estonia depended on the Soviet Union for much of its energy.

With restoration of independence the situation changed dramatically. Trade patterns were permanently disrupted, either because markets disappeared or because previously agreed contracts were abrogated and financial difficulties in Russia translated themselves into bankruptcies in Estonia. In the agricultural sector collective farms were rapidly run down. Collectivisation had been somewhat reversed in the mid 1980s but the process was accelerated following restoration of independence, and of course this sector was particularly affected by the breakdown of trading patterns with the Soviet Union.

As a result of this major economic shock, industrial production fell by about one-third between 1991 and 1992. There was in addition a very sharp rise in inflation. With the fourth quarter of 1991 as the base year (100) the consumer price index increased to 1 241 for the same quantity in 1992, and to 2 469 by the end of 1994.[4]

The economic adjustment was all the greater because of necessary changes in economic policy adopted by independent Estonia. The move to a market economy required very substantial restructuring and Estonia has pursued tight fiscal policy and, since restoration of independence, a full liberalisation of trade. After weathering a banking crises in 1992-93, 1994 and potentially in 1997-98, the banking system has been consolidated and stabilised through a substantial role of foreign strategic investments. Privatisation was initiated on a small scale in 1992-93, a privatisation law was enacted in 1993, and, by 1998, privatisation was almost complete.[5] All three Baltic States pursued strong fiscal policies during the early transition, but Estonia was the first to take decisive action. This could not have been possible, in the view of the OECD economic review, without broad political consensus that tax reform and improved control of expenditure was necessary to achieve a successful transition to a market economy.[6]

The economy began to stabilise and accelerate in the mid-1990s. Extremely rapid economic growth, characteristic of the year 1997, continued in the Estonian economy also in the first half of 1998. Estonia experienced a short-lived stock market boom in early 1997 and within six months GDP increased by 7.4%. Between June and August 1997, stock prices doubled and turnover quadrupled before collapsing equally rapidly in the final quarter of that year.

The economic climate in the second half of 1998 was, however, totally different from early 1997. The Russian financial crisis in the second half of 1998 compounded the earlier impact of the collapse in the financial markets and the related banking crisis. Growth in GDP (see Table 5) was 10.6% between 1996 and 1997, but only 4.7% between 1997 and 1998. In the first quarter of 1999, GDP decreased by 3.9%. There was an increase in the number of bankruptcies and enterprise liquidation. This, in turn was reflected in an increase in registered unemployment. The Russian financial crisis had its greatest impact on enterprises that mostly exported to the Eastern market (mostly food and chemical industry), and on the financial sector. The worsening global economic environment led to higher interest rates and this, coupled with continuing labour market problems, retarded domestic demand.[7]

These developments have shown the structural weaknesses that the spectacular economic dynamism of 1996 and 1997 had blurred. By 1998, the Baltic economies remained heavily dependent on trade with the Commonwealth of Independent States (CIS), and Russia in particular. CIS markets accounted for 21% of exports for Estonia compared to 19 and 35% for Latvia and Lithuania, respectively.[8]

Estonia's fast reorientation of economic relations to western countries and progress toward EU accession, according to the Ministry of Economic Affairs, mitigated the influence of the Russian crisis and low inflation has created a different situation for the Estonian economy in comparison to recent years. The stabilisation of prices and salaries has been favourable. The problems are in the decrease in demand in foreign and domestic markets.[9]

The Statistical Office of Estonia reported in June 2000 that in the fourth quarter of 1999 the decline in the economy stopped and was replaced by an

Table 4. **Activity as share of GDP, 1991, 1994 and 1998**

Activity	1991	1994	1998
	Percent of GDP		
Agriculture	18	11	7
Industry and construction	40	30	29
Services	42	50	64

Source: OECD, Baltic States: A Regional Economic Assessment, Paris: OECD, Figure 32,
p. 142 on the basis of data from the Statistical Office of Estonia.

upward trend in the 1st quarter of 2000. Preliminary data show the growth in GDP was 5.2% in the 1st quarter of 2000 compared to the 1st quarter of 1999.[10]

The extent of the changes in the economy from 1991 to 1998 is illustrated by shifts in sectors of the economy contributing to GDP. Agriculture declined from 18 to 7%, and industry and construction from 40 to 29%.

Significant variations in these patterns have occurred among Estonia's regions and these differences have important implications for the labour market and education policy. The OECD economic assessment characterised the situation as follows:

> "Estonia illustrates well the contrasts existing at the regional level and how they are related to sectoral or enterprise restructuring problems. Indeed, Estonia can be roughly divided into three types of regions. First, the city of Tallinn and its

Table 5. **Gross domestic product by years**

	Gross Domestic Product by Years		
	In current prices (million kroons)	At 1995 constant prices (million kroons)	Change compared with previous period %
1993	21 609.6	39 827.2	
1994	29 644.7	39 030.7	-2.0
1995	40 705.1	40 705.1	4.3
1996	52 445.9	42 297.0	3.9
1997	64 323.7	46 789.0	10.6
1998	73 325.3	48 995.7	4.7
1999*	75 360.2	48 468.5	-1.1

*Estimate
Source: Statistical Office of Estonia

vicinity has had an extremely rapid growth. Then non-enterprise regions, such as the Kohtla-Jarve/Narva agglomeration and former Soviet military bases, with heavy industrial enterprises still in need or reorganisation and restructuring. Lastly, the regions are mostly dependent on agriculture, fishing and forestry. The three different types of regions are to some extent mirrored in the distribution of non-native Estonian speakers in the population."[11]

The labour market

Changes in employment broadly paralleled the output changes since the restoration of independence. Total employment fell by about 200 000 between 1989 and 1997, with the greatest part of the fall coming in the period up to 1993. Virtually every industrial sector experienced a decline with the largest absolute reduction coming in agriculture where the 1997 employment of about 53 000 was barely one-third of the 1989 figure. Manufacturing fell from about 215 000 to about 144 000. Other sectors to show large relative reductions were mining and fishing. There were some growing sectors, though still relatively small in absolute terms. These tended to be where new activities were required by the market economy such as trade, and the financial sector.

A number of additional points may be made about the structure of employment. First, as might be expected there has been a sharp decline of over half in public sector employment, and an increase, though not so marked, in private sector: the state is still the major employer in utilities, education and health care. Secondly, there has been a slight fall in the proportion of women in employment in 1989. Thirdly, employment reductions were not evenly distributed throughout the country. The agriculture contraction affected particularly the rural areas in the south and east of Estonia, and heavy industries tended to be in the Northeast near the Russian border.

Unemployment

There are currently in Estonia, as in many other countries, two different methods of measuring unemployment. One is the number of people unemployed and registered, or claiming benefits, with the national labour office. The other is the survey method along International Labour Office methodological guidelines, which counts the number of individuals looking for work within a reference period, whether or not they are registered, and who are available to take up a job. The problem about tracing the pattern of Estonian unemployment since restoration of independence was that neither of these measures was in existence during the Soviet period. Unemployment then was not acknowledged since people were in effect guaranteed a job in some part of the state machine, and the substantial amount of "real" but disguised unemployment resulted in low productivity. Very useful research has been carried out in Estonia using a variety of sources, including the 1989 population census and retrospective surveys of individuals, and this has enabled some judgement to be made about the trend of unemployment.

Contrary to what might have been expected from the fall in output and employment, unemployment in Estonia did not show the large immediate increase on restoration of independence that occurred in some countries of the former Soviet Union. Survey-based unemployment seems to have rather drifted up during the 1990s. There are however two reasons specific to Estonia why this conclusion is somewhat misleading. First, there was substantial net emigration in the period immediately following the break-up of the Soviet Union. Some of the large state enterprises had in effect imported their labour force from the Soviet Union and when these enterprises were run down, many workers returned to Russia. Secondly, and more important, since it is a major factor in the labour market context for education and training, there was a sharp fall in activity rates. In the period between 1989 and 1997 the number of people in the labour force who were not looking for work increased by some 80 000, most of this increase coming in the period 1989-1994. By 1998 it is estimated that the proportion of the working age population who were inactive was over 30%. One reason for the increase in activity rates is undoubtedly the unpromising job situation that led to many "discouraged" workers, who saw little chance of finding work and so

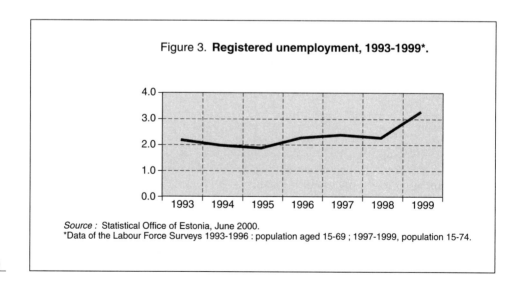

Figure 3. **Registered unemployment, 1993-1999*.**

Source : Statistical Office of Estonia, June 2000.
*Data of the Labour Force Surveys 1993-1996 : population aged 15-69 ; 1997-1999, population 15-74.

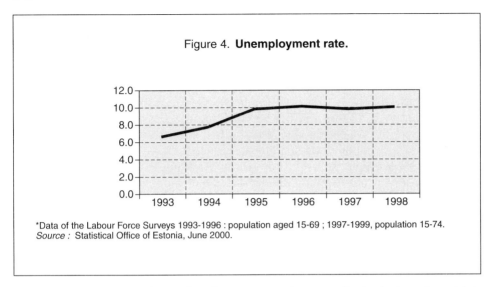

Figure 4. **Unemployment rate.**

*Data of the Labour Force Surveys 1993-1996 : population aged 15-69 ; 1997-1999, population 15-74.
Source : Statistical Office of Estonia, June 2000.

stopped looking. Another related reason is the very limited time for which unemployment benefit is paid which means that unemployed people may have lost touch with the labour offices which are an important source of job advice.[12]

The two measures of unemployment usually show differences in any country, but in Estonia the difference is very large. Survey-based unemployment is broadly three times as high in percentage terms as unemployment based on registrants at labour offices. As shown in Figures 3 and 4, the unemployment rate established by the most recent Labour Force Surveys, was 9.9% in 1998.

Figure 4 does not show the likely impact of the Russian financial crisis. Preliminary data from the Statistical Office of Estonia suggest that this rate has increased sharply to 14.8% in the first quarter of 2000. The data in Figure 3 on registered unemployment show a sharp increase in the rate of those who registered as unemployed.

Because these data are reported on a monthly basis, one can see that the rate dropped to a low point of 1.9% in August 1998, the month of the Russian crisis, and then increased steadily in the subsequent months to a high of 3.5% in April 1999. The rate has declined slightly since that time and was at 3.1% in April 2000.[13]

The main reason for the difference between the unemployment rate and registered employment rate is probably the structure of the unemployment benefit system. Benefit is paid by the labour offices to registered unemployed people, quickly if their unemployment is involuntary and after two months in other circumstances. Benefit entitlement ceases after six month's unemployment, and the level of benefit is very low by international standards. The current amount is about one-third of the minimum wage, and about 10% of the average wage. This has implications for policy which are discussed below, but it is clear that unemployed people have little financial incentive to remain on the register after six months, and there may not be much incentive to register at all if people are working in the black economy. A survey last year estimated that 13% of jobs were in the black economy. Making due allowance for the differences, both measures of unemployment are useful in looking at differences in the structure and distribution of unemployment, which have significance for the education and training system.

The review of the economy for the third quarter of 1999 prepared by the Ministry of Economic Affairs noted that the difference between the registered unemployed and actual unemployed at that point was nearly double. The Ministry indicated that the limited allocations for unemployment benefits do not motivate job seekers to register as unemployed. The Ministry observed that the unemployment rate occurred later than the decline in exports and production because of a belief that the loss of the Russian market would be only temporary. Many workers worked part-time and the number of employees did not decline substantially. The Ministry cited a report by the Estonian Economic Research Institute that every third person questioned had been unemployed at least once and 20% had been unemployed for a longer term (or 1-year). The Ministry anticipates that over the next three years (2000 through 2002), the realisation of two structural problems in the labour market will bring:

- a decrease of employees in large enterprises and their movement to successful small enterprises.

- a reduction of the share of the low paid labour force and an increase of the share of the highly paid labour force.

The Ministry also projected an increase in the number of employees in metal industries, finance, insurance, housing and catering sectors and fisheries, and a reduction of employees in mineral production industry, chemical industry, energy sector, gas and water supplies industries, transport and communications sectors and agriculture. (Study of labour force demand, carried out in Q2.).[14]

Reflecting the points about regional disparities mentioned above, there are substantial regional differences in unemployment. The counties containing the two main conurbations, Tallinn and Tartu, had unemployment rates below the national average on both measures. The rural counties had rates above average because of the decline of agricultural output and in some cases the collapse of major employers. Even more badly affected were those in the north-east which had been badly hit by structural change associated with the break-up of the Soviet Union. For example, Ida-Viru county, which includes the town of Narva where some of the heavy industries were sited, had a rate more than 50% above the national rate.

About one third of the labour force is non-Estonia in terms of ethnic origin and language. They have an unemployment rate more than twice as high as Estonian speakers do. To some extent, this is because of the concentration of Russian speakers in the heavy industries that suffered most in the industrial changes since restoration of independence, but other factors are at work. Since 1989 Estonian has been the sole official language and this has had effects on the job market. Most public sector jobs require fluency in Estonian and tests were introduced to ensure that existing workers were able to speak Estonian to a sufficient degree. Now, someone who has relevant skills but inadequate Estonian will find this expanding sector of employment closed. Private sector employers may also apply this kind of condition. Non-Estonian unemployment is obviously concentrated in the areas where non-ethnic populations were largest, but the disproportion exists throughout the country: the review team was told that non-Estonians made up 77% of the unemployed registered with the Tallinn labour office.

One other aspect of the structure of unemployment may be briefly mentioned. First, female unemployment is lower than male. This is hardly surprising given the decline in male-employing heavy industry, and the decline in labour force participation by women. Secondly, long term unemployment, at about one-third of total unemployment, is considerably lower than in many transition economies, and indeed some EU countries have a higher proportion. This suggests that most unemployment spells in Estonia are of relatively short duration, though if unemployment remains high or drifts upwards, the proportion of long term unemployed is likely to increase. Thirdly, as is commonly the case, less skilled workers are disproportionately represented among the unemployed, and the very rapid restructuring of the Estonian economy has exacerbated the skill mismatch between unemployed people and the job market. Analytical work carried out in Estonia suggests that there is a major problem of structural unemployment, across geographical, industrial and skill parameters.[15]

Notes

1. Estonia In Your Pocket, June 2000 (*www.inyourpocket.com/Estonia/Estonia_basic.shtml*).

2. Statistical Office of Estonia, June 2000 (*www.stat/ee*) .

3. United Nations Development Program, "Estonia's opportunities and human development rankings", Estonian Human Development Report 1999, Tallinn: UNDP, 1999, pp. 12-13.

4. Statistical Office of Estonia.

5. OECD, Baltic States: Regional Economic Assessment. Paris: OECD, 2000, Table 5, pp. 29-31.

6. OECD, Baltic States: Regional Economic Assessment. Paris: OECD, 2000, Figures 24 and 25, p. 82.

7. OECD, Baltic States: Regional Economic Assessment. Paris: OECD, 2000, Figure 4c, p. 46.

8. OECD, Baltic States: Regional Economic Assessment. Paris: OECD, 2000, Table 32, p. 186.

9. OECD, Baltic States: A Regional Economic Assessment. Paris: OECD, 2000, Figures 6 and 7, p. 52.

10. Statistical Office of Estonia, News release No. 61, June 6, 2000.

11. OECD, The Baltic States: A Regional Economic Assessment, Paris: OECD, 2000, p. 141.

12. Eamets, R. at al., Background Study on Labour Market and Employment in Estonia, Tartu 1999.

13. Statistical Office of Estonia, June 2000.

14. Ministry of Economic Affairs, Estonian Economy. The Quarter in Review, 3rd Quarter 1999, pp. 3-4.

15. Eamets, R. at al., Background Study on Labour Market and Employment in Estonia, Tartu 1999.

Chapter 2

Estonian Education System

Legal Famework

The Law on Education of the Estonian Republic (*Eesti Vabaariigi Haridusseadus*) was adopted on 23 March 1992, setting forth the general principles of the Estonian educational system.[1] The law enunciated the following general goals of the system:

- To promote the development of personality, family and the Estonian nation, as well as of national minorities, of Estonian economic, political, and cultural life and of nature preservation in the global economic and cultural context.

- To educate loyal citizens; and

- To set up the prerequisites of continuing education for all.

In the period since 1992, Estonia has made step-by-step progress in establishing and refining the legal framework for the education system. Other significant laws include:

- The Law on Basic and Upper Secondary Schools (*Põhikooli- ja gümnaasiumiseadus*) of September 1993, setting forth the conditions for establishing, operating and closing state and municipal primary schools, basic schools and gymnasia, as well as the principles governing basic and general secondary education.

- The Law on Adult Education (*Täiskasvanute koolituse seadus*) of November 1993, setting forth the legal conditions for training adults, along with legal guarantees for lifelong learning in accordance with the wishes of the persons concerned.

45

- Law on Universities (*Ülikooliseadus*) of January 1995. This law sets forth the conditions for establishing, operating and closing public universities, along with the principles governing higher education in accordance with the curricula of diploma and bachelor studies, and masters and doctoral studies.

- The Law on Organisation of Research and Developmental Activity (*Teadus-ja arendustegevuse korralduse seadus*) of March 1997 setting forth the basic principles governing activity to ensure the future development of creative science and technology as an integral part of Estonian culture and economic life.

- The Law on Vocational Education Institutions (*Kutseõppeastuse seadus*) of June 1998 setting forth the conditions for establishing, operating and closing state and municipal vocational education institutions, along with the principles governing vocational secondary and higher education, in accordance with vocational higher education curricula.

- The Law on Private Schools (*Erakooliseadus*) of June 1998, setting forth the conditions for establishing such schools as the property of private individuals or legal entities, together with the principles for operating these institutions and the requirements for education that the schools deliver.

- The Law on Applied Higher Education Institutions (*Rakenduskõrg-kooli seadus*) of June 1998 setting forth the conditions for establishing, operating and closing state applied higher education institutions, as well all the principles governing higher education in accordance with the curricula of vocational higher education and diploma studies.

- The Law on Pre-School Childcare Institutions (*Koolieelse lasteasutuse seadus*) of March 1999 setting forth the conditions for establishing, operating and closing pre-school institutions in municipalities, as well as the principles governing the pre-school education system.

Policy structure and governance[2]

The Parliament (*Riigikogu*) approves the laws regulating education, through which the main directions of education policy and the principles of school organisation are defined. It also approves tuition fees. The Government of the Republic (*Vabariigi Valitsus*) decides the national strategies for education, approves the national curriculum for educational institutions, establishes salary scales for educational staff and draws up rules for registering children in compulsory education.

According to the Constitution, education in Estonia is supervised by the State. The Laws on Pre-school Childcare Institutions, Basic and Upper Secondary General Schools, and Private Schools stipulate that national supervision of their activities must be carried out in line with rules established by the Ministry of Education. The Ministry of Education (*Haridusministeerium*) is responsible for:

- Co-ordinating the implementation of education policy.

- Ensuring the satisfactory implementation of – and compliance with – educational legislation.

- Drafting the requirements for the general content of education and the national curriculum.

- Establishing the rules on national supervision and ensuring that they are satisfactory; accrediting and issuing licenses to educational institutions and financing them in accordance with the law on the national budget.

- Enforcing the financial norms for use by institutions in the design of local and school budgets.

- Supervising administration of the methodological services of institutions.

- Preparing the Government-planned training of staff in education; and

- Administering the public assets used by public educational institutions and the education system as a whole.

The Ministry of Education is assisted in defining its policy by different consultative bodies as follows:

- The General Education Management Board (*Hariduskorraldusnõu-koda*), the consultative body of heads of regional educational departments.

- The Student Advisory Chamber, (*Õppurite Nõukoda*) a consultative body for the Minister, consisting of secondary, vocational and university student representatives and their organisations.

- The Educational Forum (*Haridusfoorum*), an advisory body of different interest groups discussing development issues in education.

- The Higher Education Advisory Chamber (*Kõrghariduse Nõukoda*), a consultative body of university representatives at the Ministry, which is concerned with problems of university education.

- Research and Development Council (*Teadus- ja Arendusnõukogu*), a consultative body chaired by the prime minister.

- The Estonian Science Foundation (*Eesti Teadusfond*), a consultative body of experts, concerned with financing science projects.

- Higher Education Evaluation Council (*Kõrghariduse Hindamise Nõukogu*) responsible for the accreditation of higher education institutions.

Figure 5 Displays the organisational structure of the MoE.

The county governments (*maavalitsus*) and their structures include the departments of education, which provide supervision at regional level of the educational activities of pre-school childcare institutions and schools. They formulate the education development plans of the county, provide information on public financing to the Ministry of Education, organise events for pupils and teachers in the counties and advise local government on educational questions.

The local government authorities (*vald, linn*) organize maintenance of pre-school childcare institutions, basic and secondary schools, schools for extra-curricular activities and school libraries. They also run cultural centres, museums, sports centres and other local institutions in the municipality or town concerned. In addition, the local government authorities keep registers of children in the compulsory education age-range, monitor their attendance, and appoint the heads of municipal educational institutions. Local governments draw up and implement plans for the development of regional education, define and approve school districts, appoint school boards and run school medical services and meals.

During the transition from centralised decision-making and financing to decentralised decision-making at local government, school and county government level, increasing importance will be attached to negotiations entailing a comprehensive analysis of the educational institution network. Issues involved include:

- The placement of the student population living in the area.

- The need for education at different levels.

Figure 5. **Structure of the Estonian Ministry of Education.**

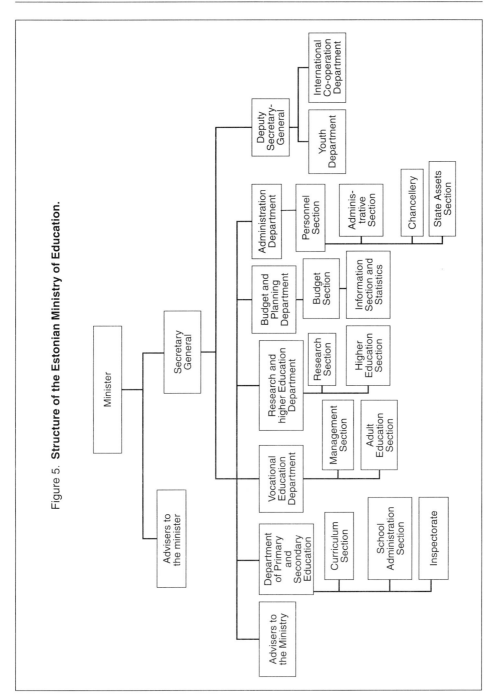

Table 6. **Pupils and students in the regular education system, 1994/95 to 1998/99**

Education Level	1994/95	1995/96	1996/97	1997/98	1998/99	Change 1997/98 to 1998/99
Full-time general education	212 375	214 562	215 501	217 501	217 577	76
Grades 10-12 (13)	31 838	31 848	32 402	33 105	32 179	- 836
Part-time general education	6 275	6 498	7 016	6 585	6 083	- 502
Grades 10 12 (13)	5 012	4 999	5 443	5 304	4 926	- 378
Vocational education	16 614	16 946	18 091	18 563	19 387	824
Professional secondary education	11 192	12 492	13 392	12 753	11 803	- 950
Higher education	25 483	27 234	30 072	34 542	40 621	6 079
Higher education : Diploma programmes	5 793	6 063	7 772	10 481	14 997	4 516
Bachelor's degree and equivalent	17 376	17 959	18 770	20 489	21 731	1 242
Master's degree and equivalent	1 926	2 588	2 803	2 673	2 822	149
Doctor's degree and equivalent	388	624	727	899	1 071	172
Total	271 939	277 732	284 236	289 714	295 216	5 502

Note: In 1994/95 to 1998/98 correspondingly, 166,381,342,230 and 255 students studied simultaneously in the evening school of general education and in vocational education institutions.
Source: Statistical Office of Estonia, Haridus 1997/98, Table 1.1. p 20.

Table 7. **Further studies of graduates from daytime secondary general school (Gümnaasium) in 1993- 98**

	1993/94	1994/95[1]	1995/96	1996/97	1997/98	1998/99
Graduates	8 569	6 650	8 787	9 435	9 551	9 216
Vocational education	863	780	929	1 094	910	1 003
%	10.1	11.7	10.6	11.6	9.5	10.9
Post secondary technikal education	1 179	995	1 485	1 804	1 449	1 198
%	13.8	15.0	16.9	19.1	15.2	13.0
Total higher education	3 411	2 652	3 539	4 235	5 031	5 856
%	39.8	39.9	40.3	44.9	52.7	63.5
Diploma studies	990	650	1 016	1 614	2 046	2 597
%	11.6	9.8	11.6	17.1	21.4	28.2
Bachelor studies	2 421	2 002	2 523	2 621	2 985	3 259
%	28.3	30.1	28.7	27.8	31.3	35.4
Total higher education	5 453	4 427	5 953	7 133	7 390	8 057
%	63.6	66.6	67.7	75.6	77.4	87.4

1. Smaller number of secondary school graduates in 1994 was a result of the addition of a 12th grade to the schools with tuition in Russian
Source: Ministry of Education

- The qualifications of teachers working in the region.

- Curricular proposals and trends in regional schools.

- Basic teaching materials in schools.

- Consistency with established teaching and cultural traditions; and

• Consistency with the social needs of regions, and the role of schools in their educational and cultural development.

From 1988 to 1996, the structures for the administration of education in Estonia were repeatedly reorganised. The Ministry of Education, the Ministry of Higher Education and Post-Secondary Technical Education and the Vocational Education Committee were combined into one Educational Committee. In 1989, the Education Committee was reorganised to create a new Ministry of Education, to administer general, vocational and higher education. The next reorganisation (in 1993) led to the establishment of the Ministry of Culture and Education which had to deal with overall education policy, higher education and science, while the State School Board (*Riigi Kooliamet*) had to deal with general and vocational education. In 1996, the Ministry of Culture and Education and Riigi Kooliamet were reorganised and a separate Ministry of Education was re-established.

Background of Estonian education system [3]

Early history

The development of education in Estonia has been influenced by countries that have ruled over its territory. The XIIIth century may be regarded as a starting point of school education in connection with the conquest of Estonian territory by German, Swedish and Danish feudal landlords. The first schools in this region were established in the largest towns. In the second quarter of the XVIth century the ideas of humanism reached Estonia from Germany, further stimulating the development of the Estonian national school.

In 1617, during the course of the Swedish-Polish war, the territory of Estonia was incorporated into Sweden and Estonia remained under the rule of the Swedish king *Gustav* II *Adolf*. This era was especially favourable for the development of education and in 1632 the Tartu Grammar School was reorganised and given the name Academia Gustaviana. This is regarded as the beginning of the University of Tartu. In the XVIIth century there were only students of Swedish and Finnish origin in this institution, and no native Estonians. The Academia Gustaviana operated until 1656, when the area was occupied by Russian troops; it again operated as the Academia Gustaviana-Carolina from 1690 to 1710 until forced to close by the Great Northern War.

An especially important event for the development of education in Estonia was the re-opening of the University of Tartu in 1802. Many outstanding scholars received their education there, including the first native Estonians.

The Republic of Estonia (1918-1940) badly needed to have a well-educated population of its own. This necessity led to the opening of gymnasiums and seminaries as well as to the extension of a network of higher education institutions. In 1919, instruction in the Estonian language was introduced at the University of Tartu and it has remained the language of instruction ever since. During this period, a number of new higher education institutions were established in Estonia: Tallinn Technical University (as Special Technical Courses – 1918), Estonian Academy of Music (as Tallinn Higher Music School-1919), and Tallinn Pedagogical University (as Tallinn Teacher Training Seminary - 1919).

After the occupation of Estonia by the Soviet Union in 1940, the introduction of the Soviet education system began and possibilities for developing independent education policy were very limited. Nevertheless, despite the pressure to adopt the Soviet educational structure and curricula, the Estonian educational system maintained Estonian as the language of instruction. While Estonian education functioned within the ideology and constraints of the Soviet education system, Estonia was permitted – especially in the 1970s and 1980s – gradually to develop more independent education policies. Textbooks were written in Estonian by Estonian authors, secondary schools had 11 years compared to 10 years in most Soviet republics. Despite the outward compliance with Soviet requirements, many Estonian teachers, especially those who received their own education and teacher preparation in the Estonian Republic (1920-1940), retained a vision of the Estonian school from earlier times.

Education renewal since 1987

As the forces for greater freedom – and evidentially, independence –began to build at the end of the 1980s, Estonia developed a strong, indigenous, grass-roots movement for education renewal – even while still formally within the framework of the Soviet Union. Change at the state-level symbolised by the "singing revolution" was accompanied by an awakening and enthusiasm for change throughout the Estonian education system.[4] The phases of the education renewal process have been described as follows:

- 1987-1989: Renewal based on enthusiasm and wide public participation resulting from relative independence from Soviet educational institutions. This included – to a certain extent – an opportunity for independent activity, self-determination in curriculum and learning organisation through school-level decisions and widespread participation in forums on educational renewal. Brainstorming sessions through the 1989 Forum of Culture and Education and the Council of Education in 1989-1991 were precursors of what would become the Estonian Education Forum in the mid-1990s. Through the state teacher in-service training system, a number of schools were challenged to introduce curricular changes providing a wider range of variations and choices. Toward the end of this period, the teacher in-service training and education research systems began to change.

- 1989-1992: A period of stabilisation focused on establishing the conditions for the functioning of the education system, preparation of the necessary legislative acts and new curricula, and disintegration and/or elimination of Soviet institutions. As indicated above, the Law on Education was adopted in March 1992.

- 1992-1994: The realisation of actual independence and the resulting search for new relationships and leadership at all levels of the system. The structure, and to a varying extent, the content – of teacher training began to change toward Western models (credits and degree structure). Institutions associated with previous times, the Teacher Training Centre and the Institute of Pedagogical Research, were eliminated. During this period, important framework laws were adopted including the Law on Basic and Upper Secondary Schools, and the Law on Adult Education.

- 1994-1996: A period of striving to bring order to the education system and to take practical steps to start democratic mechanisms and shape an educational strategy. In this period, informal seminars on the philosophy of education, including a state-wide group in 1994, evolved into seminars on educational politics and the Conference on Education in 1994-1995, and to the founding of the Estonian Education Forum in October 1995. Also in this period, the Open Estonia Foundation (Soros) and other sponsors initiated projects to establish intellectual foundations for reform and prepare school leaders, teachers, and others for needed changes. Forums for schools leaders and teachers on education renewal and curriculum reform and the "schools of distinction," were important developments. In terms of legal and policy actions, formal legal basis was adopted for the changes already underway in higher education through the Law on Universities of 1995. In February 1996, President Lennart Meri launched the Tiger Leap National Programmes the goals of which are the modernisation of the Estonian education system, and creating the conditions for the formation of an open learning environment and for a better adaptation to the demands of an information society. The new national curriculum for basic and secondary schools was adopted in September 1996.

- 1997-2000: A period of movement from strategy to action. When Estonia made further progress in establishing and updating the legal framework for the education system. Laws adopted in the period include the Law on Organisation of Research and Development Activity (1997), the Law on Vocational Education Institutions (1998), the Law on Private Schools (1998), the Law on Applied Higher Education Institutions (1998), and the Law on Pre-School Childcare Institutions (1999).

Several initiatives in this period focused on strategic thinking regarding not only education but also Estonia as a small nation in a global, knowledge-based, information technology-intensive economy, which have contributed to a growing consensus across a broad spectrum of Estonian leadership about future policy directions:

- In February 1997, the Tiger Leap Foundation was established through the leadership of the MoE, computer companies and private individuals.

- In 1997, a first effort was made to shape the so-called "Estonian Scenarios 2010" which, under the leadership of a task force of the Estonian Education Forum, would later lead to the "Estonian Education Scenarios 2015". A consensus developed supporting the scenario of "Learning Estonia", aimed at uniting society and stimulating the country's innovative capability – through a secondary approach called "interactive Estonia."[5]

- The Academic Council convened by the President of the Republic of Estonia presented a report to the *Riigikogu* in February 1998, and, then, issued a joint statement on November 19, 1998, entitled "Learning Estonia."

- The Educational Forum '98 in November 1998 concluded that, in order to develop into an open learning society, Estonia needs to take a fast and quantitative leap forward in education. The forum concluded that the "mainstream of this radical change is moving from the industrial era's state-centred system of education to the information era's society-cent-red one, to be accompanied by a substantial change in educational para-digms."[6]

- The Education Strategy document was compiled by the MoE in 1998.

At the time of the OECD team's initial visit to Estonia in April 1999, efforts to develop a synthesis of several initiatives to develop a strategy document were underway.

Estonian education system

The Estonian education system and information on the relationship to the ISCED/97 levels are presented in Figure 6. The system structure has been revised recently, especially on the levels beyond secondary education, to move toward Western systems and to reflect the Bologna Joint Declaration. As discussed in Chapters 4 and 5 of this review, discussions are continuing about the need for further clarification – especially at ISCED levels 4A and 4B and 5A and 5B.

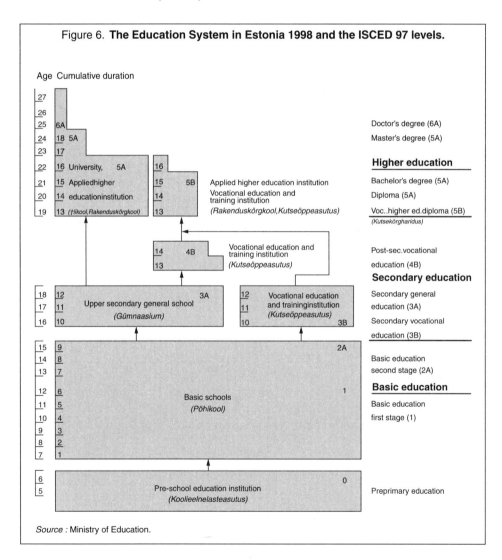

Figure 6. **The Education System in Estonia 1998 and the ISCED 97 levels.**

Source : Ministry of Education.

Enrolments and student flow

In the period from 1994/1995 to 1998/99, the total number of students in the Estonian education system grew from 271 939 to 295 216 – an 8.6% increase. As shown in Table 6, enrolments increased in higher education by 59.4%. In the same period, enrolments in general education, vocational education, and professional education remained essentially stable with year-to-year fluctuations. As discussed in Chapter 5 on higher education, State funding increases have not kept pace with higher education enrolment and an increasing proportion of the cost of higher education is being borne by students through fees.

As reflected in the enrolment trends, in the past five years, the proportion of graduates of daytime secondary general education going on to some form of higher education has increased dramatically – 63.6% in 1993/94 to 87.4% in 1998/99. The proportion going on to post-secondary technical education has remained stable.

In 1998, 70% of pupils completing Basic School continued their studies in gymnasiums with the goal of pursuing a university degree. Only 30% pursue vocational education. These patterns are illustrated in Figure 7.[7]

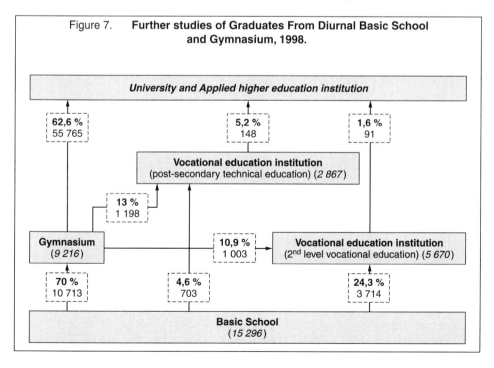

Figure 7. **Further studies of Graduates From Diurnal Basic School and Gymnasium, 1998.**

Financing

As shown in Table 8, the State budget for education in 2000 was 2 887.7 million EEK or 16.2% of the State budget, excluding capital investments and science expenditures. Education expenditures represented 7.3% of GDP in 1998. From 1997 to 2000, the relative shares of funding for the different education sectors changed slightly. The share for municipal schools increased from 40.2% in 1997 to 41.9 in 2000. At the same time, the shares of state funding decreased for universities, applied higher education institutions, and vocational education and training institutions.

Table 8. **State Budget, Public Expenditures for Education, and Education Expenditures as per cent of Gross Domestic Product (GDP), 1997-2000**

	1997	1998	1999	2000
Riigieelarve (milj.krooni)/ State budget (EEK, million)*	12 512.0	14 967.5	17 571.5	17 789.0
Hariduse osa riigieelarves (milj.krooni)/ expenditure on education in State budget (EEK, million)**	2 011.4	2 360.2	2 785.0	2 887.7
Municipal schools	809.0	1 008.7	1 211.2	1 210.2
Universities	468.3	521.7	612.8	594.8
Applied higher education institutions	95.9	102.7	116.6	111.0
Vocational education and training institutions	333.6	380.3	437.5	429.9
State schools	139.7	158.1	176.7	177.9
State Student loans	26.7	30.2	60.0	60.0
Other expenditures	138.2	158.6	170.1	303.8
Public expenditure on education as percentage of total public expenditure***	17.6	18.1		
Public expenditure on education as percentage of GDP***	7.2	7.3		

* State budget expenses do not include social and health insurance budgets.
** Expenditure on education does not include capital investments and science expenditures.
*** Public expenditure on education does include expenditures from state budget and from local budgets and capital investments, science costs and expenditures on kindergartens.

Source: Ministry of Education.

Notes

1. Ministry of Education. Structure of the Education in Estonia, final draft prepared for Eurydice, Tallinn 1999, pp. 1-3. The descriptions of laws in this chapter are drawn largely from the draft Eurydice report.

2. Ibid., pp. 6-11.

3. Ministry of Education, Estonian Academic Recognition Centre. Higher Education in Estonia: 2000 edition, Tallinn, March 2000, draft.

4. Ene-Silva Sirv, 1999. Political and Social Transformations - Analysis in the Estonian Context. In Moving Horizon in Education. International Transformations and Challenges of Democracy. Edited by Hannele Niemi. Helsinki University Press, Helsinki. Pp. 39-65. The discussion of the development of educational renewal in Estonia draws extensively on this work by E-S. Sarv.

5. K. Loogma, R. Ruubel, V. Ruus, E. S Sarv, and R. Vilu, "Estonia's Education Scenarios 2015," Eesti ühiskond ja haridus - 2015, Tallinn 1998.

6. Estonian Educational Forum Council's main standpoints concerning Estonia's strategy of education, summary of the Education Forum '98, November 20-21, 1998.

7. Ministry of Education, Information and statistical division

Chapter 3

Pre-School and Primary and Secondary General Education

Description of the system

Legal framework

Several laws establish the rights of children and adolescents to be educated and delineate the extent of compulsory education. These include the Constitution of the Republic of Estonia; the Law on Education of 1992, the Law on Basic and Upper Secondary Schools of 1998, and the Law on Pre-school Childcare Institutions of 1999. A legal requirement of the Ministry of Education is to provide an education to all children living in Estonia according to their abilities, including children with special needs. In Soviet times, it was believed that some children, because of their differences or disabilities, should not be educated. However, the situation has since improved, as the prevalence of this understanding is diminishing. In contrast to the past, Estonian legislation now supports the education of children with disabilities.[1]

Pre-school education[2]

Pre-school institutions are governed by the 1999 Law on Pre-School Childcare Institutions. The aims of pre-school education are: to support the development of children according to their abilities and interests, to instil values in children; and to teach them basic skills for learning at school and for their whole life. However, it is not compulsory to attend pre-school in Estonia. The parent or parents have the responsibility to ensure that a child has an adequate primary education and local municipalities are required to maintain the pre-schools and offer a variety of types of primary education.

Pre-primary institutions are for children aged up to age 7. In order to improve their children's readiness for basic school, most parents of 5-6-year-olds try to make the most of opportunities offered by pre-school establishments. Special school preparation groups are also quite common, although attendance at them is not a pre-condition for entry to the first grade.

Pre-primary school groups are based on the age of children, as follows: 1-2 years, 2-3, 3-4, 4-5 and 5-6, with 7 the upper age limit; sometimes, combined groups bring together children of different ages. Groups are not based on children's level of personal development. Evaluation is informal and plays no part in the possible transfer of children from one group to another.

Special pre-school learning groups and institutions support children who have problems with their eyesight, hearing or speaking, or who have physical or mental handicaps. The number of children in these groups is usually smaller. In addition, family advice centres have been established to run regular rehabilitation sessions for children unable to attend pre-primary institutions.

The number of pre-school children in classes immediately preceding basic school is greater than in pre-school classes for the very youngest. The local authorities determine the size of classes, which are usually co-educational. The maximum class size is determined by law.

Basic school and upper secondary schools[3]

The March 1992 Law on Education established compulsory secondary education in grades 1-9 (normally corresponding to ages 7-15/16). Compulsory education begins in the first full school year after children have reached age 7. However, students whose seventh birthday is in September begin school in the same September. Compulsory education continues until students have satisfactorily completed basic education, or have reached the age of 17.

Since 1992, changes to the basic school system have been introduced in parallel to the design of the 1996 national curriculum. The Estonian educational system now does not differentiate between primary and lower secondary education. Basic school is treated, as an entire unit culminating in a specific level of qualification that, when completed satisfactorily, should equip school-leavers to become citizens, and choose the next stage of their studies. The changes will be completed when the revised national curriculum is fully implemented in the year 2001. Implementation is occurring in stages, beginning in 1997 for grades 1, 4, 7 and 10, 1998 for grades 2, 5, 8 and 11, and 1999 for grades 3, 6, 9 and 12. Thus the first children to experience the new curriculum through the whole of their compulsory education (grades 1-9) for the first time are expected to end their basic schooling in the year 2006. Those who complete all 12 grades (basic and secondary) of the new curriculum will do so for the first time in 2009.

After satisfactorily completing basic school, pupils are entitled to continue their education free of charge in upper secondary education schools (gümnaasium) or vocational education institutions (kutseõppeasutused).

Financing

Pre-school education

Pre-school education institutions receive their funding from the local budget, parents, and donations (from institutions, enterprises, organisations, and individuals). Parents may contribute to teaching and catering expenses in a proportion decided by the local authority. The amounts parents pay in fees can be means-tested at the discretion of local councils. The maximum amount parents pay per child cannot exceed 20% of the official minimum salary but the Ministries of Education and Social Affairs determine the level of these expenses. The salaries of teaching staff, school heads and their deputies, and the expenses for textbooks, are covered by the budget of the Ministry of Education, in accordance with the number of students in each school.

A pre-primary school may share premises with the primary grades of basic school. The local government executive also determines the timetable of institutions, in accordance with parental needs.

Basic schools (compulsory education) and upper secondary general education

The MoE budget finances the salaries of teaching staff, school heads and their deputies and the expenses for textbooks for all schools, regardless of their ownership, up to the end of upper secondary education, in accordance with the number of students at the school concerned. All other expenses are borne by the authority responsible for the school (whether the central government, a municipality or a private concern).

Schools are under three types of ownership:

- State schools financed by the central government budget.

- Municipal schools financed by the local government budget and also by the central Government, through the Ministry of Education. and

• Private schools financed by their owners.

Schools have their own budget, which includes funds for major or minor construction work, and expenditure for running costs and the salaries of staff other than teachers, heads and deputy heads.[4]

Institutions, enrolments and teachers

Pre-school

Pre-school institutions

The number of children in pre-schools is declining in keeping with demographic changes but not in response to the actual needs of children. In 1998, 49% of all children from 0 to 6 years of age attended kindergarten, but the percentage varies greatly from region to region. In Tallinn and in Ida-Virumaa County, 64 to 65% of all 0-6 year olds were registered in kindergarten but in Tartu and Pärnu Counties, about 50% were registered, and in Jõgeva and Põlva Counties, only 27% to 28% were registered. With the higher rate of unemployment in the first half of the 1990s, many children were left at home, especially in rural areas. As a result, the number of schools declined substantially. Today, the tendency in many places, and especially in towns, is for mothers to take their children to kindergarten as soon as possible because they are afraid that staying at home with their child will result in their job loss. Therefore, in some regions there is a shortage of places for children in pre-schools.

In the last few years, many new forms of education and care have emerged, including private kindergartens, children's centres, groups to help children with special needs cope and parental counselling sessions. Many schools also organise preparatory classes for 6 year-olds who have not been to kindergarten. About one-tenth of all 6-year-old children join these groups.[5]

As of 31 December 1997, 58% of children aged between one and six attended pre-school institutions, while for those aged less than three the percentage was 27%. For five and six-year-old children, the ratio was 72%.[6]

Pre-school teaching staff

In pre-school institutions, music teachers and physical education instructors are employed in addition to the core teaching staff whose training seeks to impart the necessary theoretical and practical skills. It emphasises the importance of familiarity with the early development of children and the environment in which it occurs, bearing in mind individual needs and character on the one

Table 9. **Pre-school institutions, teachers and pupils, 1992-1997**

			1992	1993	1994	1995	1996	1997
Number of Institutions			698	656	663	671	667	670
Teaching staff	Full- and part-time	Both sexes	8 698	8 163	8 093	8 090	8 070	7 953
		Female	8 685	8 144	8 078	8 070	8 058	7 933
Pupils enrolled	Full- and part-time	Both sexes	57 269	58 495	58 271	58 743	57 020	55 077
		Female	27 927	28 690	28 844	28 449	27 662	26 688

Source: European Commission, Eurydice, Supplement to the Study on the Structures of the Education and Initial Training Systems in the European Union, May 1999, p. 18.

hand, and familiarity with the demands of the curriculum on the other. It also stresses the need to approach teaching creatively. The content and organisation of training are conditioned by the goals of subsequent education, and the need for readiness to accept changes in social circumstances and design further study activities accordingly. Staff, who are generally full-time, are trained for degrees and diplomas in higher education institutions, including universities. Since there is no firm contractual obligation for staff to attend additional training courses, opportunities for further training of pre-school teaching staff are at the discretion of individual institutions.

Strengthening pre-school education

The Open Estonia Foundation (OEF), in collaboration with Tartu University and the MoE, undertook an initiative in 1994 to draw on lessons from the Head-Start programme in the USA for the benefit of Estonia. This initiative subsequently was organised as the Step-by-Step programme through which 21 kindergartens throughout Estonia implement the "Soros pre-school program." The initiative included training of managers and teachers' assistants, development of study aids to be introduced in pre-schools throughout Estonia, special equipment for pre-schools, and conferences on parental involvement. The MoE approved the programme as an alternative choice for kindergartens.

As indicated above, Estonia enacted a new Law on Pre-School Childcare Institutions in 1999. Among the changes in that Law are strengthened requirements regarding the qualification of pre-school teachers, including a requirement that teachers be educated at the higher education level. The MoE's strategy platform for 2000-2004 recognises the importance of pre-school education. The document emphasises that a favourable footing for the child's development is created in early childhood through the supportive development appropriate for the child's abilities and interests, through stimulating interest towards learning and a creation of prerequisites for acquiring speaking, arithmetic and writing skills. As of 2000, governments have to guarantee places in kindergartens for 5-7-year-olds and for 3-7-year-olds by 2002. The government also implemented in 2000 a policy of parental payments for municipal kindergartens based on a sliding scale reflecting ability to pay.[7]

Because of the significant disparities in the size and fiscal capacity of local governments, the OECD team emphasises that these governments will be able to assume greater responsibility for pre-school education only if they are given adequate financial and technical support from the state. The annual subsidy for continuing education of teachers starting from 2000 is a step in that direction.

Basic and upper secondary general education

There were 722 diurnal (day) general education institutions in Estonia in 1998/99. The number of schools increased in the early years after independence was re-established – from 641 in 1990 to 742 in 1995, principally at the primary and basic school levels, but since 1995 the numbers have decreased.[8] In 1998/99, the schools included 180 primary schools (either grades 1-3, 1-4 or 1-6) including those with pre-school grades, 307 basic schools (grades 1-9), 235 secondary schools and gymnasiums, and 4 schools for handicapped children.[9] Of the total of 722 institutions of mainstream education, 34 were centrally administered, the municipalities ran 660 and 28 were privately maintained.[10]

In 1998/99, there were 217 577 pupils in grades 0 to 13. Of these, approximately 85% were in compulsory education through grade 9 and the others mainly in grades 10 through 13.[11] Three quarters of the schools were in towns, a proportion that has remained stable over the past decade [12]

The average number of pupils per class was 23 in 1998/98; however, as shown in Table 10, that number varied significantly by grade level and between schools in towns and those in the country. The numbers also varied by county. In several counties, there were only an average of 13 to 14 pupils per class for grades 0-13, with small numbers at some of the grade levels.[13] The overall ratio of pupils per teacher has declined slightly in recent years as shown in Table 11.

Basic schools operate in one or more shifts. The great majority of pupils at basic school study during the day, although, as indicated below, about 2% attend evening classes.

Table 10. **Pupils per class by grade level, 1998/99**

Grade level	Average	Towns	Country
0 - 4		26	17
5 - 9		27	16
10 - 13			2719
0 - 13	23		

Source: Statistical Office of Estonia, Haridus 1998/99, table 2.30 and 2.31, pp. 62-63.

Table 11. **Pupils and teachers, grades 1-9, 1996/97-1998/99**

	Pupils	Teachers (estimated)	Pupils/Teacher
1996/97	185 145	14 216	13.0
1997/98	185 710	13 913	13.3
1998/99	186 665	14 807	12.6

Source: European Commission, Eurydice, Supplement to the Study on the Structures of the Education and Initial Training Systems in the European Union, May 1999, p. 22.

An increase in the number of small schools in the early 1990s was followed by an increase in the number of combined classes which has posed new problems, such as the grouping of children of different ages in the same classroom. For example two pupils may be involved in grade 1 learning, one in grade 2 work, while three more may be trying to manage with grade 4, all of them under the supervision of a single teacher who will not normally have been trained to cope with this kind of situation. At present, such classes exist in most smaller basic schools, mainly in rural areas. Local government authorities are facing serious financial problems, because these schools have a relatively small number of pupils, but relatively high operational expenses. In spite of the developed school network, transport between home and school may still be a problem, especially for older pupils – schools with lower secondary grades tend to be located farther from homes than those with primary grades.

Enrolment in part-time basic and upper secondary education

In 1998/99, a total of 6 083 students were enrolled in part-time general education, of whom 2 297 (38%) were enrolled in correspondence study. Nineteen schools were classified as evening schools. Most part-time students (81%) were enrolled at levels beyond compulsory education at grade levels 10 through 12. Students over age 26 constituted only a small percentage (2.5%). Most of the students (65%) were 17 to 20 at the end of or shortly after the normal ages for completing upper secondary education. A significant proportion (18.6%) of the students enrolled part-time were ages 21 to 25.[14] This perhaps reflects the need of students who have finished only compulsory education and may already be in the labour market (or seeking employment) to increase their knowledge and skills.

Teachers and school directors

Characteristics of teachers and school principals

As Table 12 shows, there were 19 458 teachers in Estonia in 1998/99. Most of these teachers were in general education schools at basic or upper secondary levels. There is a bimodal distribution of teachers in terms of age and length of service.

The highest concentration is of teachers with more than 15 years of service, but approximately 20% of the teachers have less than five years of service. This suggests two challenges: first, the need to prepare young teachers to enter the profession and retain them beyond the first few years, and second, need to retrain teachers who have been in the field for a long time.

The comparatively high percentage of teachers in the first two to five years of service as compared to those in the range from five to 15 years of service may indicate a high level of attention in the first years of teaching. This, in turn, may be an indication that young teachers may be inadequately prepared for teaching, may face a negative school culture dominated by older teachers, and/or may not have sufficient support (mentoring) in their early years. The current proposal (see below) to reform pre-service teacher education in Estonia would address this problem by providing a one-year "internship" or practice period following formal training supported by a mentor or "master teacher".

To obtain a teacher's diploma, the student must follow a curriculum corresponding to the framework curriculum. This gives a person the right of access to the teaching profession. Persons who apply to teach in any other level of school than the level noted on their basic diploma must fulfil the corresponding additional requirements – via initial or in-service training. The qualification requirements for teachers specify the level of education and speciality training (speciality studied, including additional specialities, further training). Persons who do not possess the required qualifications may sign a one-year employment contract only. [15]

As shown in Table 12, a significant percentage (approximately 21%) of the teachers have education no higher than professional or general secondary. The proportion with higher education has been increasing slowly over the past decade – from 76% in 1993 to 79% in 1998/99. Approximately 33% of all teachers have preparation that is inadequate for the speciality in which they are teaching.[16] According to the new teacher qualification requirements, all teachers must have higher education as of September 1, 2002.

Teachers' contracts and wages

A teacher may work as a full-time employee or, on agreement, as a part-time employee. If the workload is 25% greater than full-time, a separate contract for an additional position is signed. Depending on qualifications, effectiveness of work and length of service, a teacher is appointed to the position of: junior teacher (junior vocational teacher, junior kindergarten teacher, etc.), teacher (vocational teacher, kindergarten teacher, etc.), senior teacher (senior vocational teacher, senior kindergarten teacher, etc.) and teacher-methodologist (vocational teacher-methodologist, kindergarten teacher-methodologist, etc.). A teacher is appointed to the one position, regardless of the number of subjects taught; the position is valid in all institutions of the same type. Teachers undergo attestation by the director of the institution, or an institutional or inter-institutional attestation commission, or an attestation commission established by the Ministry of Education.

On the basis of qualifications and length of service, the MoE has established 34 salary levels for educational workers. These salary levels apply for teachers and directors with higher education. The salary for a certain level must not exceed the minimum salary of the next level. Salaries for teachers and directors with post-secondary technical education are 20% lower than the salaries of their

Table 12. Teachers by Gender, Age, Length of Service and Education Credential, 1998/99

Category	Number	Gender and Age Female / Male			Gender and Age			Length of Service		Without Higher Education Credential
		Number	Under 30 per cent	Over 49 per cent	Number	30 per cent	Under 49 per cent	Over years per cent	0 - 5 years per cent	>15 per cent
Teachers (1)	19 458	16 092	12.1	33.6	3 366	13.4	37.3	19.9	51.6	21.5
General Education										
Full-time	16 571	14 079	12.3	32.5	2 492	14.1	27.7	19.4	51.3	4.1
Part-time	348	299	8.4	55.2	49	8.2	53.1	16.1	62.9	0.9
Headmaster/principal	606	314	3.2	46.5	292	3.1	41.4	8.3	70.1	5.8

Note (1) Total number of teachers includes vocational education teachers.
Source: Statistical Office of Estonia. Haridus 1998/99. Tables 6.3, 6.6, and 6.8, pp. 228-239.

colleagues with higher education. The salary for a deputy director (instruction and education) is 5-15% less than the salary of the director and the salary for a head of a department is 15-25% less than the director's. A class teacher has a salary 5-15% higher than a subject teacher, and the salaries for special teachers are 1.2-2 times higher. Teachers in regional priority areas (north-eastern Estonia, small islands) have higher salaries (20-30%), as do state language teachers.

A recent ordinance gives the school director more flexibility in increasing the salary of a teacher of Estonian as a second language. It is also important to abide by the ordinance entitled "Qualification Requirements for Pedagogues", and the ordinance regarding compulsory levels for knowledge of the Estonian language.

Fifty percent extra of the salary paid for a certain level can be paid for additional tasks and for effective results. The director also has the right to pay one-off additional payments and bonuses that are not limited by the restrictions described above. This gives the director an opportunity to motivate teachers.

The salary of a teacher at a basic, upper-secondary or vocational school (monthly salary and additional payments) is established in a salary list at the beginning of study year. The basis of this list is the state curriculum and the salary fund allocated to the educational institution.

In the case of distance learning in basic and upper-secondary schools, the number of teaching positions is determined based on the verbal and written assessments established in the national curriculum. If the number of assessments done by a teacher is greater, additional salary is paid at the end of the study year as hourly wages. One-off additional tasks are also reimbursed as hourly wages. Hourly wages are calculated as the salary divided by the average number of working hours per month. For a 40-hour general work week, the average number of work hours per month is 169.6; for 30 hours, it is 127.2, for 35 hours, it is 148.4 hours per month.

In basic, upper-secondary and vocational schools where the language of instruction is not Estonian, the monthly salary for teachers of Estonian is increased depending on their qualifications and years worked in the school. The employer, within the limits of general working time, pays additional salary for extra tasks (up to 0.25 extra) set.

The director of an institution establishes in the employment contract for each teacher the hours of direct instruction, the general working time and salary level.

In addition to annual vacation (56 calendar days), educational staff may take study vacations. For participation in level education, study vacations totalling 30 calendar days during the study year may be taken, and to complete level studies, extra study vacation may be taken as follows:

1. to acquire basic education, 28-calendar days.

2. secondary education, 35 calendar days,

3. higher education, 42 calendar days, for defending a master's or doctoral thesis, 49 calendar days. In addition to the study vacation, the employee also has a right to seven calendar days unpaid leave per annum. For participation in work-related training, an employee has the right to 14 calendar days per annum for study vacations, with his or her average salary. For participation in non-formal education, an employee has the right to an unpaid study vacation of 10 days per annum.

An employee who takes a study vacation related to level education is provided with his or her average salary for 10 days per annum, according to the Adult Education Act, and for the remaining of the vacation the current minimum wage is paid.

Table 13. **Full-time teachers' minimum salary, 1994–1999** (EEK per month)

Position / year	1994	1995	1996	1997	1998	1999
Not-qualified teacher	737	955	1 395	1 650	2 030	2 654
Junior teacher	1 061	1 387	1 845	2 330	2 860	3 739
Teacher	1 242	1 620	2 115	2 490	3 060	4 000
Senior teacher	1 729	2 251	2 415	2 830	3 480	4 549
Teacher-methodologist	1 841	2 404	2 920	3 210	3 950	5 163

Source: Republic of Estonia, Ministry of Education

Table 14. **Average gross teachers' wages per month compared to monthly gross wages for all economic activity, 1997–1999**

	1997	1998	1999
Õpetajate keskmine palk/ gross teachers wages (EEK) Riigi keskmine palk/	3 408	3 718	4 440
Average monthly gross wages by economic activity total	3 573	4 125	4 300
Average monthly gross wages in education	2 794	3 370	3 762

Source: Republic of Estonia, Ministry of Education

A special share (around 3% of the amount earmarked for teacher salaries) of the state budget is allocated for in-service teacher training. The Ministry of Education allocates part of the money for centrally run training, while another share is used for locally maintained training. The in-service teacher training system covers Estonian-speaking as well as Russian-speaking schools, although separate courses in Russian are organised regionally for primary school teachers. But most of the nation-wide subject courses are in Estonian.

Minimum salaries for teachers have been increasing, as shown in Tables 13 and 14 and Figure 8.

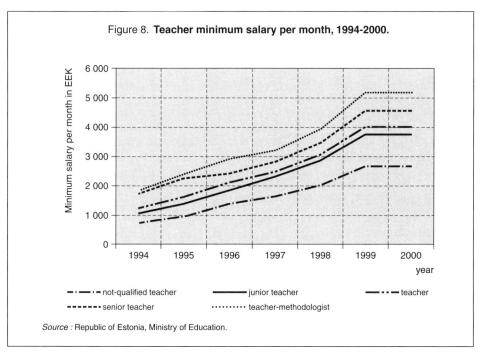

Figure 8. **Teacher minimum salary per month, 1994-2000.**

Source : Republic of Estonia, Ministry of Education.

Curriculum

Pre-school curriculum

The National Curriculum for Pre-school Education governs the work of pre-school institutions as well as providing the basis for family advice services. Rather than regulating the time spent on specific activities, the curriculum defines the fields, subject matter, knowledge and skills that have to be presented to or acquired by children. A pre-school institution is entitled to draw up its plan of activity and daily work schedule, in accordance with national tradition and the cultural peculiarities of its region. The local government authority determines which language should be used in institutions employing only a single language for their classes.

Teaching staff are responsible for methods of instruction and materials used in support. Institutions have to establish rules for the effective evaluation of teaching and children's progress, in accordance with curricular requirements.

In comparison to the 1980s, pre-schools have become significantly more "open", with greater emphasis on personal contribution of family. The role of pre-schools is to support and complement the family contribution, by promoting the growth, development and individuality of children. Several novel practices have emerged, including family care, the setting up of "integration" groups (in which children with special needs are able to mix with other children and develop alongside them while remaining close to home), family advice services, and the establishment of private kindergartens and centres for children.

Basic and Secondary Education Curriculum

The Estonian National Curriculum for Basic and Secondary Education covering grades 1-12 was approved by the government and became law on 6 September 1996. A transition to a more pupil-centred school has begun via the curriculum design process. This implies that pupils and teachers are co-operating partners, providing the former with increased freedom of choice and greater responsibility for their study results.

The Ministry of Education has also approved two levels of simplified curricula, for children with minor mental handicaps and for children whose handicaps are more severe.

In schools using the Estonian language, implementation of the national curriculum began in the autumn of 1997. Implementation started in grades 1, 4, 7 and 10, was continued in 1998 for grades 2, 5, 8 and 11, and will be completed by the end of the 1999/2000 academic year.

In 1997, on the initiative of the Ministry of Education, the development plan for Russian-medium schools was prepared as part of the 1997-2007 Activity Plan for a unified Estonian education system. The government on 22 January 1998 approved the development plan, and the Russian-medium schools began their transition towards the curriculum in the autumn of the same year.

During preparation of the national curriculum, the aim was to increase local influence on decision-making within the school organisation, as well as on teaching methods and financing, and to make schools more open. The transition to this new curriculum entails and emphasises several priority directions of development and, in accordance with the aims laid down in its general section, the content of general education and teaching materials is constantly being renewed.

Work on devising the national curriculum began in the Institute for Educational Research, at the initiative of the Ministry of Education, immediately following independence in 1991. The development of the national curriculum reflects the aims chosen by Estonia and the preferred development of its schools as well as world-wide trends in education. Teachers, teacher trainers and education officials have all been (and will continue to be) involved. In 1994 and 1995, two draft versions of the curriculum were released for discussion. Approved in September 1996, the national curriculum lays down the basic principles of schooling, providing a framework for the organisation of teaching and course content for all institutions of general education, regardless of the language of instruction. Schools base their individual work programme (the school curriculum) on the national curriculum. The development of the latter has resulted in scope for greater initiative on the part of schools, in which students and teachers can co-operate more closely. Pupils and students are freer to choose and are therefore more responsible for their results. As to the school curriculum, the teaching staff, with the approval of the headmaster and the school supervisory body, draws this up.

Drafting and determining the national curriculum falls within the jurisdiction of the Ministry of Education. The national curriculum, however, is to be seen as a framework, upon which individual schools base their own specific curriculum. Schools need to specify the content of the compulsory topics/subjects they will teach as well as the content of the elective subjects they choose to offer. In drafting the syllabus for religious education, schools should respect the wishes of students and their parents.

In 2000, a special research and development unit was established by Tartu University. The purpose of the curriculum development center is continuous development of curricula on national level by bringing together education researchers, curriculum experts and teachers.

The national curriculum provides a list of compulsory subjects with a syllabus (list of subject content) and study time (number of lessons) for each subject. The curriculum provides directions for optional subjects and requirements for completing stages of education (stage I: grades 1-3; stage II: grades

4-6; stage III: grades 7-9; stage IV: gymnasium) and school (primary: stages I-III; secondary: stage IV).

The National Curriculum consists of the following sections:

- General Goals. A list of general attitudinal "goals" (e.g. "respect of home and family") and affective goals (e.g. "love their homeland"), and a set of functional skills (e.g. "obtaining and using information").

- General Principles. A set of general criteria for teaching in Estonian schools that should be reflected in school curricula, such as "equal opportunities for receiving education" and "humanism and democracy". The general principles emphasise the responsibility students should take for their own learning and the fact that this should prepare them for their future life as a citizen of Europe and the world. The learning tasks should focus on the capacity of solving problems, making choices and taking decisions.

- Connections between different subjects. The National Curriculum identifies four themes that should be addressed in all subjects: environment and traffic safety. Furthermore, all subjects should contribute to career guidance by making clear their relation to economy and professions. Finally, informational skills and the use of contemporary information technology should be part of each subject curriculum.

- Competencies. This section merely states that a link should be established between general goals and teaching goals in terms of competencies that should be the outcome of teaching (and learning). Competencies are further addressed in the Teaching Regulations section.

- Teaching Process. This section again stresses the need for students to become independent learners, and for the teacher to assume the role of planner and creator of teaching activities and motivator of students. However, 10 of the 14 paragraphs of this section have to do with assessment and grading. Different purposes and ways of assessment are described (formative, summative, oral, written), the function of state exams is given, and the necessity of informing students about grading criteria is emphasised.

Teaching regulations and stages of schooling form the next-to-last and most extensive part. The core of this section are paragraphs listing competencies that should be acquired by students at the end of each stage, the lesson plan (number of lessons per week per stage for each subject) and maximum total number of lessons per week. The competencies are very broadly formulated.

Competencies connected to "development of opinions" for the different stages may serve as an example:

- Stage I: The student understands that people, their opinions and their wishes differ.

- Stage II: the student recognises the differences between people, views, and situations and takes these into account when communicating with other people.

- Stage III: the student is able to see problems and situations form the point of view of other people.

- Stage IV: the student has a critical attitude towards mass media and mass culture.

Underlying the competencies as formulated for different stages is a specific pedagogic conception of the development of students during their schooling: starting from an orientation of the child on the relation between the I/we/ home and the home region during stage I, via the I/we/home and Estonia during stage II and the I and surrounding people and the world during stage III to the relation between the I and the region, Estonia, Europe, the world and the universe in stage IV.

The curricula of schools section outlines the consequences for the freedom and responsibilities of schools of the relationship between the National (Core) Curriculum and school-specific curricula. The new role of teachers is also emphasised (less passive, more informed about other issues that define the role of a professional teacher, more than subject knowledge alone).

Subject syllabi are attached as appendices to the National Curriculum. A brief rationale and general aims and expectations precede two Chapters that make up the body of this section. The first deals with the basic school, the second with the gymnasium. Each Chapter starts with a list of "Objectives of Teaching" (*e.g.*, in the case of mathematics: "to ensure that the student is able to understand the role of mathematics in human activity and in the development of civilisation; improves his/her abilities, intuition and creativity", etc.). Then follows a list of content issues and a list of study results. The latter summarises the outcomes of education in terms of knowledge and skills (for example, for maths: at the completion of grade 3, the student is familiar with the clock and the calendar; is able to add and subtract concrete numbers', etc.).

Assessment Standards and Frameworks

The Estonian MoE has established an elaborate system of externally set and/or administered tests, including national assessment efforts for grade 3 and 6 and national tests for grade 9 and 12 exams. The grade 12 examination fulfils the functions of both school leaving and university entrance exam, a feature that, among the Central and Eastern European countries, Estonia thus far shares only with Slovenia.

Standards

All external assessment efforts are based on the National Curriculum, which also gives guidelines for internal assessment, to be based on school-specific curricula. The new core curriculum (1996; implementation started in 1997) gives attainment targets for all subjects for grades 1-3, 4-6, 7-9 and 10-12. It is clear that these are not specific enough to be used as assessment standards. Also grade or level-descriptors are lacking. Efforts are being made to define at least a minimum level for grade 12 tests.

The National Examination Tests and National Assessment Tests ("Progress Tests") play an important role in specifying and communicating the objectives of the new core curriculum.

The law prescribes certain subjects to be examined at certain stages and gives directions for a marking and grading system (changes made in the Law on Education passed by the Parliament on 18 March, 1997). Administrative aspects are set by ministerial decree. MoE is responsible for the grade 3-6 National Assessment. The National Examination and Qualification Centre, established in January 1997, is responsible for the National Examination Tests. This centre also develops tests of Estonian as a second language, which are crucial for obtaining citizenship and public positions. Another section of this centre deals with standards for vocational education and accredits school-based exams in vocational education.

Examinations

National exams are held at the end of grade 9 and grade 12 of general education. In vocational schools there are only school exams. Grade 9 exams consist of compulsory tests for mathematics and mother tongue, and one optional test. Grade 12 national exams consist of five tests, three of which should be external and two may be school based. Of the external ones, the mother tongue test (a five-hour written essay) is compulsory. The national tests for modern foreign languages have an oral part, which is administered internally.

Different question formats are used: constructed response, multiple choice and oral. Modern foreign language tests are proficiency tests in the true sense, setting out to test all four skills. Other tests are mostly testing knowledge and algorithms in an academic context, but an effort is made to add some questions of an applied character.

Exams for grade 9 are graded on a scale from 1 to 5, with 5 being highest. For grade 12 exams, only raw scores are given. There is no cut-off (pass) score as the minimum level has not yet been determined. Passing grade 9 exams gives immediate access to upper-secondary education.

Universities accept Grade 12 exams as entrance exams. As for the moment there are more applicants than places for many (especially the more prestigious) university studies, universities have some selection procedures in place, based either on average examination marks and interviews, or on entrance tests for the major subject. The rapidly dwindling number of school leavers may influence this practice in the near future.

National Assessment Tests

The National Assessment effort began in 1997. Each year, representative samples of 1 000 students from grades 3 and 6 are tested on reading comprehension (language of instruction) and mathematics to check mastery of a pre-set minimum level. The results are analysed according to average scores for the whole population and some sub-groups related to gender, ethnicity and location (urban/rural). From 1999 onwards test and item analyses will be conducted and all schools will receive feedback on their results. Results from grade 9 and 12 tests are analysed and used in a similar way.

International Comparison

Estonia is represented in some International Subject Olympiads, and, more importantly, taking part in the IEA civics survey for age 14 and 16. Estonia is not participating in other international studies such as TIMSS or PISA.

Target populations and special needs

Language policy

Both Estonian- and Russian-language schools are treated as parts of a uniform education system. In 82% of all schools in 1998/98 the language of instruction was Estonian, 15% in Russian, and 3% in both Estonian and Russian. The highest concentration of schools where Estonian was used was in schools focused on the early grades (93% in primary schools and 85% in basic schools). In secondary schools and gymnasia, the percentage was 65%.[17] Schools where Russian is the primary language of instruction are heavily concentrated in two counties: Ida-Viru and Harju.

There are special provisions for schools whose language of instruction differs from the national language. The Law on Basic and Upper Secondary Schools (see above) provides for the extension of Estonian language instruction and a transition towards the use of Estonian as a teaching language in upper secondary general schools (*Gümnaasium*) after the 2007/2008 school year. Since the 1993/94 academic year, the study period of secondary schools using Russian as the medium of instruction has been brought into line with those providing teaching in the Estonian language, by adding one academic year to the curriculum.

In 1997, on the initiative of the Ministry of Education, a development plan for schools using Russian was prepared. Its aims are to highlight the problems facing schools that provide education in the Russian language, find ways of solving them within the formal education system, and support plans for specific activities.

The management of this process calls for a long-term development plan and radical steps in the transitional period up to 2007. Ways have to be found to offer various language acquisition opportunities and models to different age groups, while intensifying the recruitment of language teachers and providing them with in-service training.

In schools using the Estonian language, implementation of the national curriculum began in the autumn of 1997. The "Russian-medium" schools will begin the same process in the autumn next year.

Students with special needs

The State recognises that all children have an equal right to education. Children with special needs (*e.g.* children with disabilities) must be provided with opportunities for learning in special schools created for that purpose. In every county and city, commissions of specialist counsellors are responsible for advising for disabled children appropriate curriculum or school type. With parental consent, they also have the right to send children to a so-called "sanatorium school", which is a special school specifically catering to the needs of children with chronical diseases or to the special school for disabled children.

Also, upon application from the parent(s), the commission may decide to extend the period for fulfilling the educational obligation.

The establishment of classes for children with special needs within state or municipal schools is regulated by the Basic and Upper Secondary Schools Act. These class lists are drawn according to the specific health problems and disabilities of the children. Children with moderate and severe mental disabilities are taught the national curriculum in "coping schools" focusing on the development of life skills. Aside from addressing the curriculum, Estonian law guarantees children a number of rights, including the right to receive support for the development of their hobbies.[18]

In 1998/99, special education was provided for 10.9% of students at basic school level (with 2.9% attending special schools and classes). Every attempt is made to place children with only minor disabilities into mainstream schools, reserving special schools for those with more serious problems.[19]

School Attendance [20]

Parents are responsible for ensuring that their children complete their compulsory education. The Code of Administrative Offences states that a parent's failure to accept this responsibility may result in punishment.

The overwhelming majority of Estonian children and adolescents attend school. In 1998, 97.4% of all children between 8 and 14 attended school. This means, however, that more than 4 000 children did not attend school. According to Estonian educational statistics, this group comprises:

- Children with a severe developmental disorder, who do not receive a regular education.

- Children studying abroad with a temporary residence permit; and

- Children who do not fulfil their obligation to attend school.

The last group makes up about half of the group that does not attend school. The UNDP report on Children and Education cites several reasons for absenteeism. During the process of democratisation that took place after independence, many responsibilities shifted from the government to the citizen. Many students extended this notion of individual responsibility to education, arguing that a school education is no longer necessary. Some schools have even supported this attitude in order to get rid of problem students. It should also be noted that the figures above on absenteeism are approximate, and may change in the light of the recent census.

When the Russian Army left Estonia, a situation was created in which the families (and sometimes only the children) of Russian soldiers preferred to stay in Estonia. The children who stayed now face economic difficulties, which, in some cases, have caused them to be alienated from their own families and school.

Several conditions, such as unemployment, poverty, loss of property or alcoholism, can cause families to turn to the state for support. These families are unable to cope economically and socially, and are often socially isolated. Many children in these families do not attend school.

According to the UNDP study, so-called street-children comprise the most difficult group of children who do not go to school. In addition to children without a home or parents, this group also includes boys and girls who are members of a family but whose parents do not care for them. These children usually spend time with street-gangs instead of going to school. On the street, some develop an addiction to drugs and others become thieves or beggars. When the problem was first acknowledged a few years ago, Estonians were shocked by the existence of street-children; unfortunately, the problem continues to exist.

School drop-outs

The number of adolescents without a basic education (grade 9) is increasing, which is cause for concern. The main reason these students left school was because they went to work (reason provided by 40% of drop-outs, according to 1997/98 data). These adolescents decided to leave school, despite the obvious possibility that, without a basic education, they might eventually lose their jobs. The highest drop-out rate is in grades 10 and 11: among boys 4.6% and 3.1%; among girls 3.1% and 1.9%. Within basic education are highest drop-out rates in grades 9 and 8: among boys 2.3% and 1.6%; among girls 1.0% and 0.4%.

As discussed in Chapter 4, it is possible for students to enter vocational secondary education after basic school, and approximately 28.9% of those completing basic school and going on to secondary education chose vocational education in 1998. Nevertheless, these data reflect students who completed basic school. The changes being implemented as a result of the 1998 Law on Vocational Education Institutions now require that students entering secondary vocational education complete a minimum of three years of secondary education. Shorter-term training programmes that used to be available for students intending to enter the labour market shortly after basic school are no longer available. The vocational secondary education curriculum, while still providing a significant amount of practical training, must now include more general education. It was not clear to the OECD team how Estonia is currently addressing the problem of the youth who may be "falling between the cracks" of the system - especially those who do not complete basic school and, are therefore, excluded from entering basic vocational education.

Policy Issues and Observations

The evolution of education renewal in Estonia

As emphasised in Chapter 2 in the discussion of the background of the Estonian educational system, the education renewal process can be traced to developments long before formal re-establishment of independence. Rather than evolving from a series of governmental initiatives – from the centre – as in Soviet times, the renewal resulted from a largely grass-roots effort engaging thousands throughout Estonian education.[21]

In Soviet times, the strong emphasis on uniformity in curricula, standards, textbooks, and methodology across the Soviet Union meant that only limited opportunities existed for variations – and these variations had to be approved in Moscow. The possibility for teachers to create their own programmes, different curricula for different regions and schools did not exist. Active engagement of teachers in developing curricula and different educational forms was foreign to Soviet practice. New curricula were developed through official scientific, expert, and other councils, approved by Communist Party channels. Then teachers were given extensive and continuing training – through the Teacher Training Centre – and other officially sanctioned means to ensure that they could implement the appropriate curriculum and methodologies.

Estonia, however, succeeded in the 1960s and 1970s to obtain permission for several variations from Union-wide requirements. These included preservation of 11-year secondary education in contrast to the official 10 years across the Soviet Union, and permission to have Estonian authors write some textbooks to be used in Estonian schools. Also, in the 1960s and 1970s, Estonia was authorised to use a curriculum somewhat different from the Soviet Union-wide curriculum. The differences in the Estonian curriculum were in "subject-biased" classes in sciences, foreign languages, music and art. By 1986, 102 of the 205 Estonian secondary schools had some form of "specialisation" compared to less than 1% in the Soviet Union as a whole.[22]

Between the late 1980s and the mid-1990s, most formal education institutions directly related to previous times had been closed or abolished, and Estonia established the foundations for a legal framework for the educational system. A new paradigm of education emerged from the largely grass-roots networks of schools supported by the Open Estonia Foundation (OEF), and by foreign sponsors from Denmark, Germany, Great Britain, Finland, Norway, and the US, among others.

Throughout this period, the OEF played a key role in the reform of pre-school, basic and secondary education, as well as other aspects of education and Estonian society. OEF served not only as a funding source but also as a catalyst for other developing networks and projects of other sponsors, the universities, and the MoE. Among the more important initiatives, OEF in 1994 supported a series of seminars entitled "Independent School" dealing with school development, management, policy, testing, and school legislation for 170 educators from throughout Estonia. The project was sponsored by the Estonian State School Board in co-operation with experts from the United States, Great Britain, Norway, and the Netherlands.[23]

Building on the experience of the "Independent School" initiative, OEF in 1995 launched a series of seminars for school leaders on the issues of pedagogical and administrative development, managing change, and evaluation. Fifty school teams (both principals and teachers) were invited to participate. The seminars drew on the experience of the 1994 seminars as well as the expertise of consultants from Great Britain, Sweden and Finland. This initiative developed in subsequent years into a network of "Schools of Distinction" throughout Estonia that have become the vehicle for multiple initiatives in curriculum development, school renewal, and improvement of school management. For example, OEF in 1995 funded a project on training curriculum consultants because of the need to train teachers in developing and implementing new school curricula. In this project, the schools participating in the "Schools of Distinction" project all launched their own curriculum development work.[24] In 1996, the "Schools of Distinction Co-ordinating Unit" (renamed the "Schools of Distinction Development Centre" in 1997) was formed in collaboration with the British Council and other international resources. The Centre co-ordinates the work of the Distinctive Schools Association, an organisation to assist Estonian schools in developing innovative projects and implementing the National Curriculum. The OEF sponsors an annual conference of the Association involving teachers and principals from all 50 schools as well as other educators from schools, colleges, and universities throughout Estonia. An "Infocentre" of the schools of distinction was formed in 1997 to reach as many schools as possible, to improve school teams' Internet skills, and provide consultant support to schools in the change process. In 1998, the Educational Expert Council of the OEF and the Development Centre established a chat line for the purpose of engaging teachers, principals, parents, employers and others in a discussion of the future evolution of education in Estonia.[25]

In 1998, OEF supported the launching of the "Quality Management System in Estonian Schools" project, which includes a network of 40 pilot schools throughout Estonia. Quality system modules are being worked out and put into practice, and a system for internal and external school evaluation is being modernised. The intent is to extend the quality systems being worked out in the project to all Estonian schools. A Working Group for the project is made up of the chair of quality technology of the Tallinn Technical University, the Schools of Distinction Association, the MoE, Tallinn Pedagogical University, the State Centre for Testing and Qualification, and representatives of local governments. The Working Group is charged with working out a quality assurance concept for Estonia's schools, as well as the basis for structuring and grading the quality systems to be used by schools. It is also assembling the curricula for quality schooling that will be used by teams and consultants working in schools.[26]

By the mid-1990s, a degree of stability had been achieved in the national economy and the basic legal framework and new National Curriculum had been adopted. Concerns began to grow about the need for a long-term strategy for Estonian education. In 1997, the President of the Republic's Academic Council prepared a report named "Learning Estonia," making detailed recommendations on goals and priorities for reform of Estonian education. The preamble to the report sets out three points:

- Education, as a national asset, is the main source of our future and well-being, and as such it must be raised to become the focus of society's care and attention. It is possible to build Estonia as a knowledge centred society.

- Educational conditions in Estonia reveal increasingly worrying tendencies which have been brought forward by a number of parities, including the Estonian Educational Forum. The solution to the sensitive areas in education lies in the following keywords: effectiveness, adequacy, quality and justice.

- To solve educational problems, what is needed is explicit political will based on a broad social consensus, complete with an effective implementation mechanism.[27]

As mentioned in Chapter 2, a task force of the Council of the Estonian Education Forum in 1998 developed the "Estonian Education Scenarios 2015", building on the previous "Estonian Scenarios 2010". The basic premises of the 2015 scenarios were as follows:

- Estonia will certainly be an information society by 2015.

- The use of computers has become usual; the entire society has been "networked": a large part of the people's everyday communication happens via telecommunications networks; schools and educational organisations of all levels will be networked electronically; besides the "physical" network of schools there is a virtual training network.

- The present "campus" type universities have been linked to global information networks or have developed into virtual learning environments.

- In the formal education system, integration patterns in the relations with the informal education system have changed; the emergence of new strata or levels can be expected in university and postgraduate education.

The scenarios were compiled considering the combined influence of two key factors that determine the nature of society: (1) social cohesion – the degree to which society is integrated, and (2) the capacity of society to innovate – the quality and intensity of social striving.[28]

The four scenarios are depicted in Figure 9:

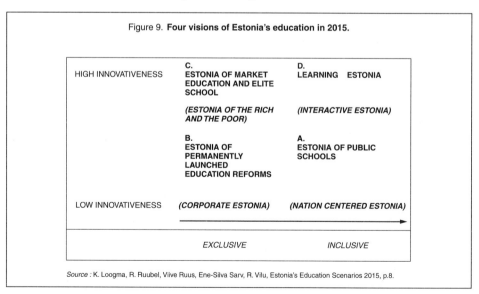

Figure 9. **Four visions of Estonia's education in 2015.**

HIGH INNOVATIVENESS	**C.** **ESTONIA OF MARKET** **EDUCATION AND ELITE** **SCHOOL**	**D.** **LEARNING ESTONIA**
	(ESTONIA OF THE RICH *AND THE POOR)*	*(INTERACTIVE ESTONIA)*
	B. **ESTONIA OF** **PERMANENTLY** **LAUNCHED** **EDUCATION REFORMS**	**A.** **ESTONIA OF PUBLIC** **SCHOOLS**
LOW INNOVATIVENESS	*(CORPORATE ESTONIA)*	*(NATION CENTERED ESTONIA)*
	EXCLUSIVE	*INCLUSIVE*

Source : K. Loogma, R. Ruubel, Viive Ruus, Ene-Silva Sarv, R. Vilu, Estonia's Education Scenarios 2015, p.8.

Excerpts from Learning Estonia Scenario [29]

Estonia is treated as a pilot country in transit to a learning and knowledge-centred society, as a country, where new ideas, technologies, new forms of economy, human coexistence, learning and teaching are being invented and tested.

Lifelong learning has developed into a lifestyle, which is integrated with nearly all activities. Estonia's learning communities serve as pathfinders in the learning and teaching sphere, also to a global extent.

Various education philosophical and pedagogical paradigms are tested in education. Particular attention is paid to the development of the child's creativity at the initial education levels and in youth.

The education-related legislation is centred around the child's and human rights. Their observance in the education system is strictly monitored.

The curricula of formal education have been developed according to general competency concerning all education levels. The need to develop a creative, reflective and motivated learner, taking the lead in his/her own studies, is particularly stressed.

Elementary, basic and general and vocational secondary education have been merged into one comprehensive – but at the same time differentiate – school, which has led to the development of individual study paths from an early age. Special attention is paid to the acquisition of varied (individual and collective) learning abilities and the development of a multi-intelligent personality.

Nearly 100% of graduates continue their studies after leaving secondary school.

The profession of a teacher-tutor-lecturer is honourable and presumes great creativity. The teacher is increasingly turning into a forecaster and designer of education and learning, therefore inevitably also of society's future: an organiser and consultant of learning.

A broad consensus in support of the scenario "Learning Estonia" developed among the participants in the Estonian Education Forum and other key leadership groups within the country. Excerpts of the scenario directly relevant to basic and secondary education are shown in the following text box.

The Education Forum similarly outlined priorities for action in late November 1998. Prior to the change in government in early 1999, the MoE was in the process of developing a strategy document intended to draw together the various proposals.

At the time of the first OECD visit in April 1999, the new Minister had been in office for only a short time. Recognising the breadth of the changes that had recently been adopted (*e.g.*, the National Curriculum and new testing and assessment initiatives), the Minister was focused on the practical aspects of implementation. The new Minister also indicated his intention to continue efforts to gain agreement on a strategy document. A final draft of the "Strategy Platform" for 2000-2004 was nearing completion in April 2000.

While the OECD team was not able to address all dimensions of reform of pre-school, basic and secondary education, the team gave particular attention to the areas of curriculum/assessment, human resource development, initiatives to prepare Estonia for information technology, and the overall efficiency and cost effectiveness of the education system. Despite the extraordinary progress of Estonia in the past decade, an underlying concern of the OECD – shared by the leaders in Estonia – is the sheer size of the task of moving from current policy and practice to the vision of "Learning Estonia".

Curriculum and Assessment

National Curriculum

The National Curriculum reflects a clear consciousness of modern educational thinking. The focus on competencies is in line with what may be found in any of the curricula in OECD countries. As with any bold new initiative, it will be necessary for Estonia to make adjustments in the National Curriculum over time. In refining the National Curriculum a number of points should be considered to reflect the changes implied in "Learning Estonia".

There is a sharp contrast between the philosophy laid down in the general part of the National Curriculum and its elaboration in the subject syllabuses. The "Objectives of Teaching" are too broad to serve as guidelines for school curriculum development. The lists of content issues and study results, which will determine the content of teaching, suggest a traditional teaching approach, focussing on conveying academic knowledge. As one person expressed it to the OECD team, "The new curriculum consists of two parts: the rationale and general philosophy, and the subject curricula. The first part is wonderful, but the subject curricula, maths and history for instance, are still strongly dominated by the past and not adapted. Reality is different from the official policy." The problem, from this observer's perspective, is that while a philosophy can be put forward by a small group, changing the reality of teaching requires mass re-training, which is exactly what appears to be lacking.

If, for example, students should be prepared to function as a citizens in a democratic society, the subject content – or at least parts of it – should be put in the context of daily life in a democratic society. This link would make clear how the subject contributes to this general goal. If this association is not made, schools will ultimately ignore the general philosophy and resume teaching as they did in the past, as indeed some stated they were already doing.

As Estonia reforms secondary vocational education to strengthen the relationships with general secondary education and vice versa, it will be increasingly important to provide students with opportunities for practical application, and to ensure that the curriculum is appropriate for the full range of students. A strongly subject-oriented curriculum, targeted to the needs of students who intend to pursue further academic study, will not provide for adequate integration with vocational curricula, and will be inappropriate for students intending to enter the labour market or further training in vocational fields.

The schools visited by the OECD team emphasised the contrast between the goals of a more integrated and student-oriented teaching, and teachers assuming new roles as well as the reality of new emphases on content and subject matter but with a lack of materials to support stronger subject-oriented teaching. In their eyes, expectations of a more integrated content oriented towards the average student, as opposed to content-ridden academically oriented subject curricula, did not come true. Another general complaint regards the friction between requirements for integrated and student-oriented teaching and the strict subject-oriented timetable in the same curriculum, which do not seem to match.

Some schools and teachers believe that new textbooks and other teaching materials should solve this problem, and complain that these are not available (*e.g.* for history: no source materials, for geography no modern maps), or that insufficient numbers of copies have been received. Others state that this change requires a great deal of re-training of existing staff, for which there are no facilities.

The OECD team is especially concerned that the National Curriculum is currently not well designed to serve students in the full range of abilities across Estonia. In other words, it is inconsistent with the goal of strengthening the knowledge and skills of all students, because the subject content can only be mastered by the top 15% of students. Most schools visited by the OECD team mention the high difficulty grade of the subject content, both in the new curriculum and in some new textbooks, as compared to the old situation.

The perspective on child development in the National Curriculum reflects a longitudinal ordering of competencies (I/we/home > region > mother land > continent > world> universe). The realities of child development, however, tend to be more concentric than linear. The national curriculum, therefore, may be unnecessarily restrictive for schools as they seek to meet children's diverse learning needs.

As a further illustration of the contrast between intent and reality, the current subject syllabi do not reflect the general principles but emphasise the role of students as passive receptors of encyclopaedic knowledge. The volume of subject content and the depth seem to be beyond the ability of average students. A reduction in the number of subjects, and deletion of issues that are of value only to those students who wish to pursue a subject in further studies, should be considered.

To increase the coherence between the philosophy underlying the National Curriculum and the subject syllabi, the OECD team recommends that Estonia clarify in the subject-specific syllabi how the general principles apply to each specific subject. A concentric rather than a linear child development model should be used in the ordering of competencies, in order to support efforts of schools and teachers to meet children's diverse learning needs. Assignments for students related to portions of the subject content should be revised to emphasise the role of students as active independent learners in order to support the general principles of the National Curriculum. The curriculum should challenge students to formulate their own questions and ways to find answers. To support a more integrated approach to teaching and learning, the National Curriculum could frame the first stage(s) of general education in terms of broad domains that cut across traditional school subjects in order to support a more integrated approach to teaching and learning.

The OECD team's visits to schools and discussions with the teachers' trade union representatives suggest that Estonia faces a major challenge in gaining the understanding, support, and re-training of teachers to fully embrace the new National Curriculum.

Unfortunately, the contrast between the general philosophy and the actual provisions of the curriculum tends to reinforce teaching approaches from earlier times. These contradictions result in confused signals to schools about the underlying intent of the reforms. Gaining support and understanding of teachers in the new paradigm of "Learning Estonia" will require that teachers be fully engaged in the curriculum development process. This approach contrasts sharply with the top down implementation in Soviet times; in-service training was structured to train teachers to follow explicit, centrally defined curricula with little if any emphasis on engaging teachers in the curriculum development process. The new paradigm requires change not only in the approach to implementation but also in the mentality of teachers, many of whom have had only limited experience with active participation in curriculum development.

The continued use of the National Curriculum as a tool for school account-ability is an illustration of the contrast between philosophy and implementation. There are clear differences between the intent of the MoE to shift to a more out-comes-oriented approach to accountability, and the reality experienced in the schools – especially in the role of the inspectorate. In earlier days there was only one curriculum for all, and therefore it could be used as a form of input control. Now the single curriculum has been replaced by a National Curriculum that is essentially a framework, within which each school has the responsibility to ela-borate its specific school curriculum.

Inspectors who were interviewed by the OECD team said that their task had shifted from controlling school work plans (lesson tables) and some in-depth study of subject teaching to making prognoses for numbers of students in clas-ses and numbers of students applying for certain university studies. In reality the role of Inspectorate is to evaluate all aspects of school activities. Inspectorate is expected to work according to the evaluation criteria approved by the Minister in 1999. To cope with this and other new responsibilities, inspectors received a two-year training course at Tallinn Pedagogical University. MoE has started also a new project on inspection with the Office for Standards in Education.

Despite initiatives for change, the OECD team is concerned that the inspectorate continues to play a role of diligent controller of formal delivery of curriculum, and is moving only slowly to new thinking. Directors from visited schools indicate that the role of the county inspectorate to monitor the delivered curriculum seems to focus on checking if schools stick to the prescri-bed timetables. This is not experienced as being very helpful. A representative from a county authority was less sure of the new understanding of county inspectors of their jobs; she remarked: "The education department of this county authority is far from pro-active: it only monitors whether the rules are obeyed." And a deputy Mayor of a big city said: "The inspectors of this county report to city government, mostly about implementation of central rules."

The OECD team recommends that Estonia move to a more outcomes-oriented approach to accountability, by focusing the role of the MoE and the inspectorate more on output control and holding the school accountable for reaching the outcomes of education rather than for using a specified and approved input. The county inspectorate should emphasise its monitoring and stimulating role, and should support implementation by reflecting on delivery by schools and advising on how to put ideas into practice.

Textbook development for the new curriculum is underway, but the OECD team had a sense that there remains a significant gap between the textbooks actually available in schools and the requirements of the National Curriculum. The MoE must authorise new versions of textbooks. The OECD team suggests that Estonia consider the efficiency to be achieved by eliminating central textbook authorisation and leaving the responsibility of making the national curriculum framework operational to educational publishers and schools. Such a free market approach may lead not only to better outcomes but also to more cost-efficient production and timely educational delivery.

Finally, the OECD team found little information on how the curriculum is actually delivered within Estonian schools. The impression prevails that quite a few teachers concentrate on making ends meet, keeping students at their tasks and not caring too much about innovation coming from above. It is important for Estonia to invest in research on the delivered curriculum and to develop better ways to support the implementation of the National Curriculum.

Assessment and Testing

The elaborate system of externally set and/or administered tests maintained by the MoE has the potential of providing all stakeholders in education with ample data for monitoring and improving the quality of education. National tests seem to provide a means for quality control, as is suggested by the following remark of a senior governmental official: "The Estonian educational community consists of many small, long-standing networks. The third year of national testing revealed dramatic differences between these. Something should be done about small gymnasiums: many of these should probably be closed down and a national network should be established." Local authorities interviewed by the OECD team seemed to regard the national exams and progress tests as instruments for evaluating schools, and in particular in identifying underachieving schools. Ironically, local officials still saw the results of regional

Olympiads (more than the national examinations) as the best indicator for school achievement.

The replacement of entrance exams by national school leaving tests is generally accepted and appreciated – at least within universities, and there appears to be a strong correlation between the results on those tests and results of students in their first university year.

The MoE intends to continue to refine the national testing and assessments. A number of issues arose in the course of the OECD review that should be considered as policies and practices are revised.

Currently, the state exams set high expectations and have a subject/discipline emphasis with the result that the tests do not allow the majority of students to demonstrate what they know and can do. The most frequent reaction on the national exams heard by the OECD team concerned the difficulty level. Schools complain that exams are far too difficult, and wonder whether the whole ability range can be served by a single exam. There are suggestions for exams to focus on the threshold of minimal competency, and to have separate exams for high achievers or students specialising in a subject. The grade 12 exams attracted most of this criticism. Meeting the high expectations of the national exams is perpetuating the problem of highly congested syllabi and curriculum overload.

The OECD team urges Estonia to recognise the need for state exams that are appropriate for the students at all ability levels as well as those for whom a less discipline/subject matter approach would be more appropriate. A broader approach is also important for those students who do not intend to pursue higher education immediately following upper secondary education. One alternative to address this problem would be to introduce exams on two levels, at least for some crucial subjects. Another alternative would be to split up certain subjects and/or their exams, *e.g.* mathematics, into content parts that are relevant for certain further studies, thereby avoiding that students have to pass high hurdles that are in fact irrelevant to their future careers.

The OECD team is also concerned that the externally set and/or administered tests may be too directive, to the extent that teachers are encouraged to teach to some targets that are predominantly tested with external tests and ignore other important aspects that could be well assessed with other instruments. Such an unanticipated effect would contradict the basic intent of educational renewal to move away from the passive, compliant teaching of earlier times toward greater teacher initiative and responsibility for curriculum and pedagogy. As one teacher observed: "In Soviet times the government used the curriculum to control what was taught. Now the government intends to use testing to accomplish the same thing."

The OECD team recommends that Estonia consider alternatives such as the following as it continues to refine its testing program:

- Re-writing the study result paragraphs of the syllabi into more specific attainment targets, and adding a section on assessment criteria, describing how mastery of the attainment targets will be assessed and against which criteria – for instance in terms of level descriptors. In this section it should be specified which attainment targets need external assessment and which may be left to some internal procedure at school level.

- Investing in developing guidelines and instruments for schools to organise internal assessment of important skills, such as active skills for modern foreign languages, or investigative skills in mathematics and sciences.

- Providing for a procedure to monitor the quality of school-based exams, which should encourage schools to undertake creative ways of assessing important skills, fostering dissemination of school-based assessment methods and making results comparable across schools.

- Developing and publishing criteria to facilitate checking validity, efficiency and effectiveness of the present exams. There are no published production and quality criteria for the national exams.

- Focussing analyses on outcomes by skills, to have a better match between the goals in the central part of the core curriculum. Schools now only receive feedback from the MoE on their examination results in terms of scores by subjects that can be compared with national scores.

- Making an effort to develop collaborative initiatives among small schools for the purpose of improving the efficiency, reliability and validity of school-based exams, *e.g.* in local networks or twinning arrangements with bigger schools. Efficient, reliable and valid school-based exams are difficult to realise in small schools.

National Assessment

The OECD team was impressed by Estonia's progress in the development of and commitment to continuing refinement of the National Assessment tests. In the course of the OECD review, several issues were raised that could be useful in the refinement process.

An important use of National Assessment results is to assist teachers and school principals to improve teaching and learning. School-level discussions related to quality can be greatly enhanced by information about the performance of the students in the school. The OECD team observed a need for a broader effort to encourage and support the use by schools of National Assessment results. The MoE published a decree on 9 April 1999 regarding principles and analysis guidelines for an external system to assess learning results, including the introduction of means for self-evaluation by schools.

Reports of the National Assessment were made available to every school in Estonia and hence should have some impact on school self-evaluation. Still the most common way of evaluating achievement continues to be to rely on judgements of individual teachers and comparing admission rates to universities, especially the more prestigious ones. Some schools that participated in National Assessment tests use the results to evaluate their own achievement with respect to a more general standard. Others felt that they could not readily use the reports to evaluate teaching and learning in their own school.

The OECD team heard concerns about the potential problems in the interpretation and application of National Assessment results. Particular concerns related to the public-oriented character of the National Assessment reports and to how they are received and used by schools and the media. For the MoE, the results of grade 3-6 national assessment, analyses of samples of grade 9 exams and full-population analyses of grade 12 exams are important indicators for the achieved curriculum. A considerable number of MoE staff is involved in setting specific tests and collecting and analysing the outcomes. Ever since the grade 12 exams have been replacing the university entrance exams, the press has become more interested in the results. Last year saw a publication of top-and bottom-ranking schools, according to their exam results, which caused considerable commotion. In 1999, the MoE published results for groups of schools that are similar according to certain benchmarks, such as ethnicity and location. For the same reason, controlling the difficulty level of exams has become an urgent issue. Maths tests, in particular, have turned out to be far above the average student level. A design is being developed for comparing difficulty levels across subjects and from one year to another.

It is important to recognise that some background variables may determine the outcomes of learning as much as teaching in schools. In the current National Assessment, the main variable, social economic status, is not controlled, and there are no longitudinal data. These gaps give schools an easy way out to explain unsatisfactory results ("our students come from a deprived area, the ability of enrolling students is low", etc.). An effort should be made to use National Assessment in the long run for monitoring the added value of teaching, and to reward and support schools accordingly.

Other suggestions from the OECD for strengthening the National Assessment process include:

- Seeking assistance as necessary from international agencies with long-standing record in organising National Assessment efforts.

- Lengthening and differentiating the tests to increase their capacity to measure validly and reliably important skills.

Joining a major international comparison of student achievement would also be helpful. The OECD team heard concerns that Estonia continues to lack adequate quality assurance mechanisms and has no reliable data that might serve to compare the level of Estonian students with those elsewhere. Apart from the IEA civics study, Estonia has not been involved in any of the major comparisons of student achievement.

Developing the human resources for education renewal

Underlying many of the interviews in the course of the OECD review was a theme that Estonia faces a major challenge in developing the human resources – teachers, school principals, and other education personnel – necessary to make the vision of "Learning Estonia" a reality in schools throughout the country. Data on the characteristics of teachers reviewed earlier in this chapter (refer to Table 12) underscore the problem. These are summarised below:

- Approximately one-third of teachers are over 49 years old and more than half of all teachers have been teaching for 15 years or more. Therefore, a significant proportion of the teachers still in the schools received their training and taught within the constraints of the policies of the Soviet Union.

- The highest concentration is of teachers with more than 15 years of service, but approximately 20% of the teachers have less than five years of service. This suggests two challenges: first, the need to prepare young teachers to enter the profession and retain them beyond the first few years, and second, a need to retrain teachers who have been in the field for a long time.

- The comparatively high percentage of teachers in the first two- to five-years of service as compared to those in the range from five to 15 years of service indicates a high level of attrition in the first years of teaching. This, in turn, may be an indication that young teachers may be inadequately prepared for teaching, may face a negative school culture dominated by older teachers, and/or may not have sufficient support (mentoring) in their early years. The current proposal (see below) to reform pre-service teacher education in Estonia would address this problem by providing a one-year "internship" or practice period following formal training supported by a mentor or "master teacher."

- Approximately 16% of teachers have professional and 5% only general secondary education. The proportion with higher education has been increasing slowly over the past decade – from 76% in 1993 to 79% in 1998/99.

- More than 70% of school principals have been in service for 15 years or more, and more than half are age 49 years or older. While one would expect principals to be more experienced than teachers, data suggest that a major challenge of not only retraining but also preparation of a large number of new principals.

- An additional complication relates to the status of teachers in Russian-language schools. Teachers in these schools generally received their training in universities outside Estonia in other regions of the then Soviet Union. As the OECD team learned in visits to Russian-language schools, the networks for teachers and school principals remain strongly oriented to Russian universities. At the same time, most teachers in Estonian schools attended Estonia universities (either Tallinn Pedagogical University or Tartu University) or an Estonian pedagogical college. Estonia, therefore, faces a special challenge of developing a common understanding of philosophy and practice across a diverse population of teachers and school leaders.

- The declining birth rate and projected enrolment decline are seen by many as an opportunity to strengthen teacher quality. Despite the lower status compared to previous times and low wages, the position of teacher remains one of the more stable sources of employment. The incentives for older teachers to retire are, therefore, not as strong as might be expected.

In-service training

The Soviet Union had a highly developed model of in-service teacher training through which teachers were required to obtain additional training at prescribed points in their careers. A structure including the Teacher Training Centre, the Institute for Pedagogical Research and a system of methodological consultation all supported the system of in-service education and policy implementation at the school level. In the period immediately following re-establishment of independence (1992-1994), these institutions were closed – if they had not already ceased to function in the changes beginning in 1987.[30]

Following grassroots development of renewal in the late 1980s, Estonia developed a highly decentralised network of relationships for in-service education and school change. A minimum of 3% of the salary fund for teachers is allocated to the MoE for in-service education. The MoE then allocates most of these funds to the municipal level (2.4% in 2000) based on the number of students in each municipality, and the remainder is retained for certain national priority initiatives. Through the Law on Adult Education, funding is also available directly to municipalities for in-service education. A substantial share of the funding comes from special projects, such as those funded through the Open Estonia Foundation (OEF), the British Council, the Geothe Institute, projects with Finland and other Nordic countries, et al. Funding also comes from the teachers themselves, targeted donations of schools and resources from the school's income and from money raised by the teachers' associations.

Prior to 1991, in-service training programmes were organised centrally and the universities and colleges were the primary providers. Now the in-service education system operates on a largely market basis with a large number of providers who compete to respond to school requests for training. The MoE approves the courses that teachers can take with funding from the state budget, but the choice of courses and approved providers is a local decision. In addition, as described earlier in this chapter, foreign initiatives have provided essential support in developing a wide array networks for in-service education and education renewal since the early years of independence.

The OECD team was impressed by the depth and thoughtfulness of the Estonian initiatives to education renewal – in-service education, curriculum development, resource networks, innovative projects, and growing use of information technology to support improvements in teaching and learning. Clearly a strength of the developments in Estonia is the widespread engagement at the school level of teachers, principals and other stakeholders in the renewal process – a legacy of the "bottom-up" renewal discussed earlier in this chapter. At the same time, the OECD team was concerned that the highly decentralised, and often fragmented, network was not sufficient to address the severity of the problems facing Estonia regarding the future of the nation's human resources for education.

At the time of the OECD review, the MoE was engaged in a review of in-service education. Reflecting on the highly market-driven provision of in-service education, the MoE made the following statement in communication to schools in early 2000 in conjunction with the draft MoE regulations on improving teachers' professional skills:

> Currently, the market of the in-service training providers is big and the quality diverse, and the teachers are still in the process of developing their knowledge and skills as subscribers to the service. Therefore, it would be irresponsible to put the responsibility for the professional development of the teaching body of a school on the shoulders of teachers themselves. Teachers should be more involved as partners in schools, in local governments, in the county, in teachers' associations, etc.[31]

In an analysis of use of state funding allocated for training, The MoE found a lack of knowledge of the training needs at all levels. Excerpts from the MoE assessment are as follows:

- In-service training of schools in the municipality is formed in a majority of cases by way of simply accepting certain offers (bids). Schools and municipalities do not act as subscribers who want to contribute to the design of the training. As a rule, ready-made training packages are bought and the choice is made on the basis of the average cost of the training day per participant. Training Guides and the Teachers' Newspaper, are known as sources of information on training but the Internet is not yet very popular. Higher schools have declared their readiness to bring training closer to the trainees, but this information is not yet available in the Training Guides.

- Alternative training providers, or so-called "project training", are becoming an ideal for participants because of the substantial contribution the trainees themselves can make, the team-work approach in several stages, diversity of methods and new (foreign) lecturers. The training financed from the projects should support the training based on the development needs of schools. Currently it seems that participation in the projects is rarely based on the school's development plans.

- The county is not informed about the different training possibilities used by the teachers, which are financed from non-state budgetary resources, therefore, priorities set at the county and national levels are based on incomplete information. The MoE still lacks an effective system for the selection of target groups for nation-wide training programmes.

- An analysis of the feedback by 812 trainees (mainly school managers and directors of studies) by the Tallinn Pedagogical University Adult Education Centre found that only 49.5% of the participants were interested in the practical implementation of the knowledge gained from training. Others participate in the training because they met nice people there. Trainees expressed a strong preference for providers other than the colleges and universities citing as reasons the passive teaching of university professors and the desire to hear "new" instructors.

The MoE concluded that if a totally market-driven approach were taken by allocating resources from the state budget for in-service training to the teachers' own disposal, the result would be to:

- Increase the number of teachers who do not participate in in-service training.

- Increase the inequality of teachers in purchasing the training service.

- Reduce the needs of schools and local governments for setting their training priorities and for designing their in-service training programmes.

- Eliminate the possibility of the county educational structures and the state to have an impact and direct the development of schools through in-service training.

In response to this assessment, the MoE has embarked on policy changes to achieve a "more targeted infrastructure and to link the training programmes more closely with the development plans of educational institutions." The mission of the MoE is defined as raising the quality of long-term training and subscribing to the so-called operational training in such areas which would contribute to educational innovations and have a long-term impact. In 2000 this is to include:

- Re-structuring of the market-based training.

- Specifying the responsibilities of colleges and universities, local institutions and training providers.

- Promoting greater specialisation and increased co-operation among training providers.

- Increasing the importance of Ministry of Education, of county and local governments as record keepers and evaluators of the training provided.

The national training priorities of the MoE for the year 2000 include: school management, quality control, use of information and communication technology (ICT) in teaching, integration (teaching Estonian as the secondary language), prevention of drug abuse, a student support movement, and teaching in combined (joint) classes.

The MoE regulations provide clear directives regarding responsibilities at each level of the state:

- At the school level, it is the task of the school manager to direct training. Budget decisions should put an emphasis on long-term systematic training (aimed at maintaining and raising the qualifications of teachers) and operational training which responds to the in-service training needs from the internal evaluation of schools, self-assessment and external assessment (regular inspections, comprehension tests, national exams).

- Teachers are to be involved in the planning of training at school, in local governments, in the county, in teachers' associations and other national initiatives. As the market of in-service training providers is big and the quality diverse, decisions on training cannot be made only on the basis of teachers' wishes.

- The county level is to provide support according to county priorities for training programmes of subject groups, support of regional training centres and participation of teachers in training projects abroad. At the county level, support is provided for regional training centres established in co-operation with the British Council and the Goethe Institute. The MoE is emphasising the development of training centres and a focus on the county as the level for co-ordination of multiple training initiatives, including those supported by the EU.

The MoE is also strengthening its quality assurance and accountability requirements for training at each level of the system, including more detailed requirements for record-keeping and internal and external evaluation.[32]

The OECD team supports the directives set by the MoE to strengthen the nation-wide co-ordination, coherence and quality of teacher in-service training. They respond to many of the concerns expressed in the course of the review about the need to strengthen the in-service education of teachers and to improve school management. As reflected in the Schools with Distinction and Quality Schools initiatives, and in the many excellent programmes supported by foreign sponsors, Estonia is clearly a leader among nations in transition in the quality and diversity of its education renewal initiatives.

Nevertheless, greater coherence is clearly needed in order to ensure that the limited resources of teachers, schools, sponsors, and the government are targeted to overcome the more serious obstacles in the Estonia's journey toward the vision of "Learning Estonia." The OECD team is sensitive to the fear that any effort of the MoE to establish greater systemic co-ordination and coherence in in-service training could lead to the re-establishment of practices of top-down systems. Therefore, opportunities for broad participation of teachers and principals and informal networks must be guaranteed.

The OECD team recommends that the MoE intensify its on-going efforts to shape and reach agreement on a comprehensive strategy for renewal of the human resources for Estonian education. Such a strategy should be consistent with the underlying philosophy of "Learning Estonia," and provide for a balance between the need for nation-wide leadership and coherence, and the need for deep and widespread engagement at the school, community and regional levels of all stakeholders in the renewal process. Following the pattern of recent years, the strategy should emphasise multiple networks, extensive use of information technology, and a high level of involvement of NGOs and other sponsors. As discussed below, a key element of the strategy should be the development of the next generation of educators through the reform of teacher education in Estonia's colleges and universities.

Teacher training

Teacher training is performed at universities or rakenduskõrgkool in the form of a diplom-study or by passing an additional one-year (40 credits) study programme after *bakalaureus or diplom-study*. The education level of a teacher depends on the institution in which he or she is employed. Most teachers in pre-school institutions and vocational education institutions are currently trained also according to the higher vocational education programmes.

Educational personnel are trained at four universities, three applied higher education institutions and two post-secondary vocational schools as follows [33] :

- Tallinn University of Educational Sciences (*Tallinna Pedagoogikaülikool*) trains pre-school, primary and subject teachers for basic and secondary school level. Teacher training offered in Diplom-study and bakalaureus-study with nominal duration of 4 to 5 years depending on the study programme.

- University of Tartu (*Tartu Ülikool*) offers qualifications in subject-matter fields for basic and secondary school levels. Teacher training is offered mainly at the university college in Narva.

- Estonian Academy of Music (*Eesti Muusikaakadeemia*) and Eesti Estonian Academy of Arts (*Kunstiakadeemia*) train teachers of music and arts.

- Other institutions offering teacher training are: *Tallinna Pedagoogiline Seminar, Tartu Õpetajate Seminar, Virumaa Kõrgkool, Viljandi Kultuurikolledž and Rakvere Pedagoogikakool.*

The OECD team gained the impression that the renewal of teacher education in colleges and universities has proceed somewhat more slowly than changes in in-service training and networks largely outside the formal higher education system. In the period from 1992 to 1994, changes were made in teacher education to reflect Western models:

- Transition from the Soviet time subject system to the system of academic credits.

- Courses and subjects of the Soviet curriculum changed as ideological subjects were excluded and new courses included such as economy, foundations of philosophy, management, and foreign languages.

- Course titles and – depending on the lecturer – content were changed.

- The system has been redesigned to reflect Western systems of credits and baccalaureate, masters and Ph.D. degrees.

- Relationships between faculties of colleges and universities and schools established by Soviet institutions such as the Teacher Training Centre, the Institute for Pedagogical Research, and the system of methodological consultation as these institutions were abolished or disappeared after independence was re-established.[34]

Estonia has also taken other actions to move all teacher training to the higher education level, to require teachers to obtain a higher education, and to link the pedagogical colleges directly to either Tartu University or Tallinn University of Educational Sciences (formerly, Tallinn Pedagogical University).

Changes in Estonian education over the past decade and, in particular, the changes implied in "Learning Estonia," require fundamental rethinking of the teacher education. The changes will be far deeper than restructuring of the content of courses. What is required is a dramatic change from traditional teacher education that is faculty/teacher-centred, discipline-oriented, didactic and taking place in a passive learning environment disconnected to practice in the schools. The new generation of programmes should be student/learner focused, emphasise interdisciplinary teacher and research and encourage integration of subject-matter and pedagogy with extensive engagement in school-based reform.

In the course of the OECD review, the team was impressed by a number of developments at both Tartu University and Tallinn University of Education Sciences that reflect the most forward thinking in reform in OECD countries. A positive sign is that leading rectors and professors are actively engaged in education reform and in deliberations about reform of teacher education – a phenomenon not always present in other countries. A specific example is the initiative on active learning sponsored by the Open Estonia Foundation aimed at developing and implementing new models of teaching and learning in schools and universities. Another example is the project at Tartu University under the leadership of Professor Toomas Tenno to develop an integrated, learner-centred science education curriculum. This project, being undertaken in partnership with several schools, allows students to identify common themes among the major branches of science as they appear in the natural world. As a result, students will be able to make connections between disciplines of physics, chemistry and biology in addition to learning about each discipline.

In the course of the OECD team's visits to schools, teachers and principals repeatedly emphasised that the colleges and universities lag seriously behind the latest developments in education in Estonia. Common concerns relate to:

- The continued emphasis on subject matter and disciplines.

- Limited interdisciplinary emphasis in either teaching or research.

- Continued use of lecturing as the primary mode of instructional delivery and little attention to active learning and other modes of teaching and learning appropriate for "Learning Estonia".

- Frequent examples of professors who continue to lecture using out-dated literature and materials.

- Limited connection of college and university faculty members with school reform (although, as indicated above, many cited specific examples of extensive involvement in reform).

- A teacher preparation curriculum that provides students with inadequate opportunities for practice and provides little or no mentoring of young teachers.

The review team recognises the complexity of the issues involved in reforming teacher education which are also being raised in many OECD countries. As universities attempt to raise their prestige in the highly competitive global knowledge economy, they face pressures to increase the emphasis on subject matter – both disciplinary and inter-disciplinary. The integration of the formerly separate research establishment within universities reinforces the tendencies already within the universities to strengthen research and pay less attention to teaching. The reward systems for professors remain strongly oriented away from the tasks critical for strong teacher education programmes: teaching and issues of pedagogy, inter-disciplinary teaching and research, applied research and practical application through involvement in the field.

At the time of the OECD review, it was clear that reform of teacher education is a major priority for the Minister of Education, the *Riigikogu* and higher education leaders. Several projects are underway to explore new models. A major change will be the requirement that teachers have a practice year or internship following completion of formal teaching training. A project is underway to train master teachers who will serve as mentors for these new teachers.

In August 1998 a "memorandum of understanding" on the reform of teacher education was developed at two seminars by a working group including representatives from six main teacher training institutions, Ministry of Education, Teachers' Union and the Open Estonia Foundation. The purpose of the memorandum was to establish a "common ground" for the forthcoming process of strategic planning for teacher training reform in Estonia. The memorandum outlines the need for reform, citing many of the issues identified above and called for a 10-year strategic plan for reforming teacher education in Estonia. The goals of the reform set forth in the memorandum are:

- Redesigning teacher education programmes in all institutions in order to meet the needs of changing society as well as contemporary educational paradigms (life long learning etc).

- Designing and implementing mechanisms for continuous curriculum development.

- Implementing new learning methods and modes in teacher education.

- Establishing a network of practice schools and trained mentors.

- Increasing the intensity and level of counselling during the school practice, raising its status to be equivalent with lectures and other on-campus instructional activities.

- Motivating teacher trainers to become involved in educational practice outside the university or college.

- Increasing the accountability of teacher training institutions by implementing new accreditation standards for teacher education programmes.

- Designing, legislating and implementing procedures for teachers' professional accreditation.

- Enhancing international co-operation in teacher education (from exchange programmes for students and teaching staff, to joint research projects), keeping balanced national and global aspects in teacher education.

The memorandum also outlines the principles of design and implementation for the strategic plan:

- The process of design and implementation of the strategic plan should be "transparent", and all stakeholders should be informed about the process.

- Constructive analysis of the current situation in teacher education, related literature, ongoing and recently accomplished development projects should be the basis for working out alternative decisions and building project teams.

- The processes and mechanisms (committees, working groups, project teams, etc.) will be specified in co-operation between all groups of "stakholders."

- The goals and objectives of the programme should be specified.

Issues to be addressed by working groups included redesign of the teacher education curriculum, the learning environment in teacher education (including ICT, new textbooks, group size and learning methods), teacher qualification standards, research programmes on teacher education and teacher education for vocational schools and for Russian-speaking schools. [35]

The OECD team understands that an agreement has been reached on the framework for significant reforms. The details of these plans were not available for the team, however. The framework requirements for teacher training have been developed in co-operation with social partners. These requirements are based on the memorandum noted above.

The OECD team endorses the basic directions outlined in the 1998 Memorandum. Of Understanding on Reform of Teacher Education in Estonia. The team recommends that teacher education reform receive the highest priority as an integral part of Estonia's strategy to develop the human resources necessary to realise the vision of "Learning Estonia."

Information and communications technology (ICT) in education

Estonia has made a significant commitment over the past decade to developing information communications technology (ICT) in education. While the focus initially was on general education, the emphasis today reaches to all education levels. The national priority is to develop ICT across all dimensions of Estonian life and economy as a core element of making Estonia competitive in the global economy.

At the beginning of the 1990s, the status of ICT, as described by a recent UNDP study,[36] could be characterised as follows:

- The infrastructure, compared to the West, was old and inadequate.

- The ICT consumer was unused to filtering or selecting available material.

- The users had little experience of interactive communication.

- The existing models for activity, service and financing were not functioning.

- Estonian academic computer knowledge was relatively high, and there was a noticeable level of interest and readiness amongst the wider public.

The UNDP study points out that the first school computer programme was implemented in the years 1987-1992. The Ministry of Education organised the provision of all high schools with one classroom containing Estonian made computers. Basic schools received 1-2 computer stations. Approximately 3 000 computers were sent out to schools. The Ministry of Education Training Centre conducted courses for teachers. The aim of the programme was to provide basic computer training for as many school pupils as possible.

This first initiative faced several practical implementation obstacles. The computers were unreliable – many broke down and were left to gather dust, according to the UNDP. It was difficult to employ computer teachers because the subject did not exist in the official curriculum. It was difficult to motivate subject teachers to make use of the computers. In spite of these problems, however, the initiative provided schools with an initial experience in the use of information technology and a large number of computer teachers and pupils went on to study information technology at university.

In 1992-1996 the Ministry of Education carried out open tenders for school computers and invested approximately 0.2 million USD annually for IT equipment. Because of the cost of the computers in comparison to teacher salaries and other expenses, it was impossible for most schools to participate but about 40 Estonian schools did manage to find the money to install proper computer classrooms. Some schools managed to progress from computer instruction to the actual use of IT equipment in school work. In other schools, there were only a few computers used by few people. IT knowledge did not generally extend to the school teaching staff. In this period, a start was made in purchasing software suitable for Estonian study programmes and adapting it to Estonian use, as well as in creating original software.

On February 21, 1996, President L. Meri proclaimed the Tiger Leap National Programme, with the goal of modernising the Estonian educational system, creating the conditions for the formation of an open learning environment and better adaptation to the demands of an information society.

The Tiger Leap Programme had the following goals:

• Providing Estonian teachers with elementary computer skills, which would enable them to use modern information technological opportunities in teaching their subjects.

• Building a distance and continuous learning structure for teachers and pupils.

• Developing a curriculum with the assistance of a learning environment which develops interactive and learning skills.

• Connecting the Estonian educational system with international information databases.

• Encouraging the creation of original software for Estonian language, culture, history and environment, in accordance with the state curriculum.

- Developing information systems for education with the assistance of the EC-Phare programme.

- Establishing regional computer training centres in every county to provide assistance for the development of information technological infrastructure of the schools.

In order to achieve these aims, the Tiger Leap Foundation was established in the spring of 1997 on the initiative of the Ministry of Education, computer companies and individuals. The working aims of the Foundation were determined to be to:

- Organise the financing and running of the Tiger Leap Foundation in co-ordination with the Ministry of Education.

- Initiate, finance and carry out other projects associated with the computerisation of the Estonian educational system.

- Participate, in co-operation with the Ministry of Education, in the development of a strategy for the Tiger Leap Foundation.

- Organise public events for explaining and promoting its activities.

- Co-operate with other entities in order to achieve the goals of the Foundation.

The UNDP study of Tiger Leap for the period from 1996 to 1998 found that the initiative had significantly improved the availability of hardware throughout Estonia. The level of approximately 50 pupils per computer was reached, compared to the goal of 20 pupils per computer, and approximately 4 000 computers installed in schools (Figures 10 and 11). From 3.5% to 4% of all teachers (700) now have a computer at home. The responsibility for hardware was shifted from the MoE to local governments and companies. UNDP found that IT resources are becoming important work resources of all teachers and pupils. The figures depict the variations in the availability of computers in the schools in each county in early 1999.

In the initial period of the Tiger Leap, there were three problems regarding software: imported software was mostly illegal, there was no study software in Estonia and there was no information about software in other languages or its suitability for the Estonian curriculum. The UNDP study found progress in overcoming each of these problems. The study found that teachers combined material from the Internet with their own work, which means that software problems are beginning to be resolved.

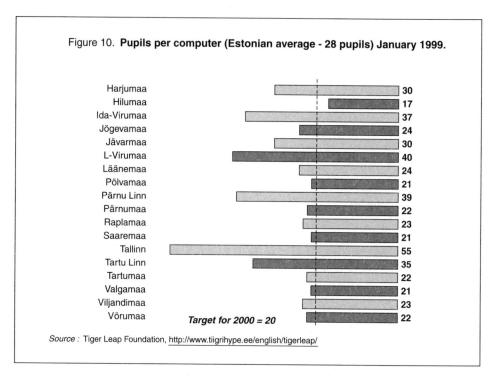

Figure 10. **Pupils per computer (Estonian average - 28 pupils) January 1999.**

Harjumaa	30
Hilumaa	17
Ida-Virumaa	37
Jõgevamaa	24
Jävarmaa	30
L-Virumaa	40
Läänemaa	24
Põlvamaa	21
Pärnu Linn	39
Pärnumaa	22
Raplamaa	23
Saaremaa	21
Tallinn	55
Tartu Linn	35
Tartumaa	22
Valgamaa	21
Viljandimaa	23
Võrumaa	22

Target for 2000 = 20

Source : Tiger Leap Foundation, http://www.tiigrihype.ee/english/tigerleap/

One of the aims of Tiger Leap is to connect all schools to the Internet. This area is receiving serious attention, but problems remain due to financing, low status and the lack of data communication related competency in the counties. The provision of Internet services for schools is the statutory obligation of the Estonian Educational and Research Data Communications Network (EENet) administered by the Ministry of Education. The UNDP study found that, in practice, data communication for schools has ended up in a no-man's-land – between the Ministry of Education and EENet and some schools use the services of commercial providers. UNDP found that 137 schools have Internet connections, and 300 schools have a dial-up facility. In other words, one-fifth of schools has an Internet connection and e-mail is used by half the schools.

A system for issuing a computer user skills certificate (AO) as a competency certificate has been initiated in Estonia, analogous to the ECDL (European Computer Driving License) programme. This certification system also enables

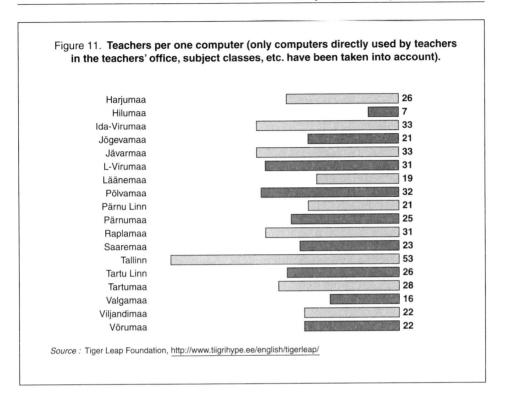

Figure 11. **Teachers per one computer (only computers directly used by teachers in the teachers' office, subject classes, etc. have been taken into account).**

Harjumaa	26
Hilumaa	7
Ida-Virumaa	33
Jõgevamaa	21
Jävarmaa	33
L-Virumaa	31
Läänemaa	19
Põlvamaa	32
Pärnu Linn	21
Pärnumaa	25
Raplamaa	31
Saaremaa	23
Tallinn	53
Tartu Linn	26
Tartumaa	28
Valgamaa	16
Viljandimaa	22
Võrumaa	22

Source : Tiger Leap Foundation, http://www.tiigrihype.ee/english/tigerleap/

the standardisation of initial training curricula. This, however, needs to be followed by the standardisation of IT managers' competency certificates and qualifications' acquisition. Most schools now have a computer teacher. Besides the universities, there is now a growing number of competent training companies. There are, however, a number of unresolved issues: the competency certificate and acquisition of qualifications are not yet standardised, nor is the curricula, the IT training for school leaders is inadequate and the training of systems administrators is only nascent.

The UNDP report identified one of the most important results of the Tiger Leap Programme should be considered the creation of a co-operation between the Tiger Leap Foundation, the MoE, the county governments, the associations of district governments, the schools and service providers.

The report also found widespread changes in actual practice at the school level that could be attributed to increased use of information technology. Communications between teachers and pupils have been greatly expanded and opened far beyond the immediate school, village or town and students' participation has encouraged more active participation and learning. The opportunity now exists for greater flexibility in developing and changing teaching tools and resources and teachers' experience has provided an opportunity for them to learn to learn – in ways that previously would not have been possible. ICT has been a catalyst for internal school change.

Overall, the UNDP study found that Tiger Leap was beginning to serve the intended catalytic role in promoting change in the education system. The study observed that the programme has concentrated mainly on the creation of an infrastructure and has been very equipment-centred. Much has been achieved, not only by the Tiger Leap Foundation, the universities and the schools, but also by the local governments, but the effect on the content of education has been relatively minor.

Rural schools and the efficiency of the school network

The OECD team heard repeated concerns about the inter-related issues of quality and funding. The issue was not necessarily one of the total funding available for education. It was more about the efficient use of existing resources. The most serious questions centred on significant disparities between rural and urban areas and, in particular, the problem of small schools and small, economically weak municipalities. The issues arose in several contexts:

- Differences in performance between students in rural and urban schools on state assessments. The differences point to the underlying problems of the inability of some schools to implement fully the National Curriculum, to undertake the necessary school-based curriculum development, provide the essential resources (textbooks, computers and other learning materials) or to carry out the necessary school-based assessment and evaluation.

- Too many small gymnasiums – institutions that will become even smaller as enrolment drops.

- Inability to reduce the number of teachers as enrolment drops – the number of teachers remains the same or, in some cases, is increasing. In the larger urban areas, officials see declining enrolments as an opportunity to reduce the number of teachers, increase class size and attract better qualified teachers. In other areas, being a teacher – even at a comparatively low wage – is one of the only sources of employment available. Reducing numbers of teachers is difficult – in fact, the pressures are to increase employment places.

- Serious problems in getting young teachers to go to work to rural schools – despite incentives of forgiveness of student loan debt.

Because of the time constraints of the review, the team had only a limited opportunity to observe directly the disparities that were reported by others. However, in the visit to one school the team had a glimpse of the stark contrast between the conditions at schools in Tallinn and Tartu and those in economically depressed areas of Estonia (see box).

Visit to a Small School

This school has 220 students in grades 1 through 12, the students coming from a catchment area with a radius of 35 kilometres. Because it is a Russian school, implementation of the new curriculum began only in 1998 and the school principal does not see the change as a step forward. The actual curriculum does not match the new expectations and what used to be taught in class 8 should not be taught in class 7, but no changes have yet been made. Textbooks and instructional materials are out-of-date and do not match the new expectations. The school received information about the national grade 9 tests and used sample items to prepare students for the first tests this year. The principal was aware of the grade 3 and 6 tests and received the MoE booklet with samples and analyses, but failed to use it for the school's own evaluation purposes. The principal criterion for evaluating the school's performance is the number of students who enrol in tertiary education. Those who do go on tend not to go to the more prestigious universities. The overall impression was a feeling of alienation and despair because of the serious threat of being closed down in the near future.

The data reveal serious challenges for Estonia. The UNDP report, Poverty Reduction in Estonia, underscores the disparities in income across the country. Local governmental units were divided into five income cases, based on Estonia's average gross salary as shown in Table 15.

The UNDP report points out that the areas with a high risk of poverty are classes 3, 4 and 5, where the income level is less than 80% of Estonia's average. These classes cover 29% of the population and 73% of the total local governments, mostly of rural districts. Except for the town of Valga (class 3), all larger towns and county centres belong to either income class 1 or 2. Those districts in direct poverty are in the so-called south-eastern and eastern Estonia depression

Table 15. **Distribution of local government units into income classes**
on the basis of 1997 gross incomes

Class	Type	Local Governments	Percent of Number of Local Government Units	Population	Percent of Population
1	Wealthy	38	15.0	838 616	58.0
2	Coping	31	12.2	194 811	13.5
3	In poverty risk	72	28.3	200 055	13.8
4	Poverty endangering coping	68	26.8	143 944	10.0
5	Direct poverty	45	17.7	67 952	4.7
	Total	254	100.0	1 445 378	100.0

Source: UNDP, Poverty Reduction In Estonia Background And Guidelines, Chapter 4, 1999 Statistical Office of Estonia, 1998.

belt (Jõgeva, Põlva, Valga, Võru and Viljandi counties). Most local government areas in this group are characterised by a small population, the dominance of the primary sector, an under-developed service sector, an age level that is above the average and a lower level of education.[37]

Local municipalities are critical elements of the Estonian education system at the pre-school, basic and secondary general education levels. There are essentially two levels of governance in Estonia: the state and the municipality. Counties are part of the national government and have only small education departments with functions (such as the inspectorate) largely delegated by the MoE. As indicated earlier in this chapter, of the 722 diurnal general education schools in Estonia in 1998/99, 660 were the responsibility of municipalities. The state pays salaries of teachers directly to municipalities based on a formula (key factors include the number of students and location of school in an urban or rural area). Local authorities may decide how many teachers to hire and whether to pay them bonuses. Municipalities are responsible for providing space, maintenance, and equipment. On average between 40 to 50% of municipal budgets is spent on education.

The reality is that many of Estonia's municipalities are too small or otherwise do not have the capacity in either fiscal or public administration capacity to assume fully their education as well as other critical responsibilities. The Estonian Constitution establishes a one-tier local government and delegates extensive powers to the municipalities. The transition from Soviet party political administration to locally governed units following restoration of Estonian independence was an important change, but it placed extraordinary new responsibilities at the local level. [38]

The 1999 UNDP report makes these observations about the situation:

- Most of the approximately 250 small municipalities in Estonia, which amount to 90% of all local government units, cannot meet these conditions... The budget funds are mainly used to preserve the existing resources – to repair roads and buildings and to pay the salaries of the people employed by the municipality.

- The present local government units are too small to provide the intellectual and economic resources necessary for development. Merging municipalities would increase competition between the elite, consolidate resources, create the minimum necessary concentration of "capital". But this does not overcome the main faults of Estonia's rural policy.

- The most acute problems have arisen in south-eastern Estonia, but the current economic and social resource and the social capital of the Estonian village as a whole are not sufficient to halt the continued deterioration of the social environment.[39]

As discussed earlier in this chapter, significant differences exist between schools in areas classified as "towns" as opposed to "country" in the numbers of pupils in each class level. For basic schools (grades 0-9), there were 24.3 pupils per class in schools in towns compared to 14.8 pupils per class in country schools. At the gymnasium level, there were 28.6 pupils per class in towns compared to 22.0 pupils per class in country schools. The differences among counties are even more severe.[40]

The discussion in the previous section of this chapter on ICT underscored the significant disparities among counties in the availability of computers and in the extent to which teachers have gained the necessary training to take advantage of new information technologies.

The OECD team recognises that the political and education leaders in Estonia are clearly aware of the many dimensions of the problems quality and efficiency in the school network. A number of initiatives are underway and others are under consideration to address the problems. For several years, the Open Estonia Foundation (OEF) has focused attention on small rural schools. In 1995 a project on effective small schools project brought together representatives of 25 schools to analyse their problems and work out ways of improving their effectiveness. A projected called "Rural School – Highly Competitive School," from 1996 to 1998 emphasised the role that schools in small towns play as centres of the intellectual and cultural life. The project focused on developing the students' skills to live in a high technology society and increase their computer skills. In 1996 and 1997, OEF supported a project providing additional training for elementary, middle grade and high school teachers in rural schools and supplying them with methodological study materials for integrating economics as an official subject into the school curriculum. This programme is a continuation of a 1996 programme, which was implemented for teaching basic economics in elementary schools in rural areas. OEF reported to the OECD team that one of their priorities in the near future will be on schools as social centres in rural areas and small towns.[41]

Policy alternatives mentioned to the OECD team included:

- Addressing the problem of small gymnasiums by developing regional, if not a national, gymnasium through which perhaps the state would assume more direct responsibility for the quality and efficiency of this level of education.

- Providing support for teachers to serve students in isolated towns and in their homes.

- Building on existing initiatives to utilise information technology and distance learning to develop networks among small rural schools, and linking these schools with resources of towns, colleges and universities, regional training centres and other resources.

The MoE has identified as two of its seven primary aims for reform as (1) increasing the efficiency of the education system and (2) promoting of social justice and creating conditions for access to quality education for all the students irrespective of their gender, regional and economic differences. The draft Strategy Platform for 2000-2004 outlines several alternatives for restructuring the schooling network in order to achieve optimal use of resources. One alternative would be to change the division of responsibility for financing schools between the state and municipalities. The responsibility for teachers and teachers' salaries and textbooks would be transferred to local municipalities making these municipalities totally responsible for financing general secondary schools. This would be accompanied by changes in tax policy to allocate an increased proportion of revenues from income taxes to municipalities. Allocations from the state-owned support fund would be implemented in order to balance the regional inequality between local municipalities.

This alternative presumably would address the major disparities in resources among local municipalities. It would focus the responsibility and provide the additional authority and financial leverage for municipalities to take measures to optimise the school network within their jurisdiction. [42]

Summary of recommendations

National curriculum

- In refining the National Curriculum a number of points should be considered to reflect the changes implied in "Learning Estonia."

- Clarify how the general principles apply to the specific subject in order to increase the coherence between the philosophy underlying the National Curriculum and the subject syllabuses.

- Provide for increased integration within general education of opportunities for practical application as appropriate to prepare students for the labour market and to provide for increased integration of general and vocational education at the secondary level.

- Give increased attention to the needs of the full range of student abilities and aspirations in contrast to a focus primarily on the needs of the top 15% of the students.

- Consider a concentric rather than a linear child development model in the ordering of competencies in order to support efforts of schools and teachers to meet children's diverse learning needs.

- Consider specifying the national curriculum for the first stage(s) of general education in terms of broad domains that cut across traditional school subjects in order to support a more integrated approach to teaching and learning.

- Revise portions of the subject content in terms of assignments for students, challenging them to formulate their own questions and ways to find answers in order to support the general principles of the National Curriculum that emphasise the role of students as active independent learners.

- Move to a more outcomes-oriented approach to accountability by focusing the role of the MoE and the inspectorate more on output control and hold school accountable for reaching the outcomes of education rather than for using a specified and approved input.

- Consider the efficiency to be achieved by eliminating central textbook authorisation and leaving the responsibility of making the national curriculum framework operational to educational publishers and schools.

- Invest in curriculum research in order to develop more information on how to support its implementation.

- Continue to reform the role of the inspectorate to emphasise monitoring and stimulating role, supporting implementation of the National Curriculum by reflecting on delivery by schools and advising on how to put ideas into practice.

Assessment and Testing

- In efforts to refine and improve the testing/assessment system, the MoE should recognise the need for state exams that are appropriate for the students at all ability levels, including those students who do not intend to pursue higher education immediately following upper secondary education.

National Assessment

- Consider lengthening and differentiating the tests to increase their capacity to measure validly and reliably important skills.

- Increase the involvement of National Assessment effort to encourage schools to make use results to improve teaching and learning.

- Increase MoE attention to the public-oriented character of the National Assessment reports and to how they are received and used by schools and the media.

- Increase MoE attention to the public-oriented character of the National Assessment reports and to how they are received and used by schools and the media.

- Recognise that some background variables may determine the outcomes of learning as much as teaching in schools. In the current National Assessment, the main variable, social economic status is not controlled, and there are no longitudinal data. This give schools an easy way out to explain for unsatisfactory results (our students come from a deprived area, the ability of enrolling students is low, etc.).

An effort should be made to:

- Use National Assessment in the long run for monitoring the added value of teaching and reward and support schools accordingly.

- Join a major international comparison of student achievement perhaps in collaboration with other transition countries.

In-service training

The OECD team recommends that the MoE intensify its on-going efforts to shape and reach agreement on a comprehensive strategy for renewal of the human resources for Estonian education. Such a strategy should be consistent with the underlying philosophy of "Learning Estonia" and provide for a balance between the need for nation-wide leadership and coherence, and the need for deep and widespread engagement at the school, community and regional levels of all stakeholders in the renewal process. Following the pattern of recent years, the strategy should emphasise multiple networks, extensive use of information technology and a high level of involvement of NGOs and other sponsors. As discussed below, a key element of the strategy should be the development of the next generation of educators through the reform of teacher education in Estonia's colleges and universities.

Teacher education

The OECD team endorses the basic directions outlined in the 1998 Memorandum of Understanding on Reform of Teacher Education in Estonia. The team recommends that teacher education reform receive the highest priority as an integral part of Estonia's strategy to develop the human resources necessary to realise the vision of "Learning Estonia".

Rural schools and the efficiency of the school network

- Place a high priority on the underlying reforms in public administration, tax policy, and economic renewal that are essential prerequisites for addressing the severe problems of small and largely rural local municipalities. Such reforms are essential foundations for the education reforms designed to improve the quality and efficiency of pre-school, basic and secondary general education in Estonia.

- Continue to recognise that schools, especially basic schools, are at the core of the social, cultural and economic survival of communities – especially in rural areas. Too often in other countries decisions about closing schools in the early grades have been made largely on economic efficiency grounds (*e.g.*, because of comparatively low student/teacher ratios) without full consideration of the broader impact. Revitalisation of life in rural, including attracting young people, is a critical priority for Estonia, and schools in the early grades will be an essential element of that process.

- Continue to strengthen the support networks for small schools using information technology and open-distance learning whenever feasible. The initiatives already underway supported through the Tiger Leap Foundation, the strengthening of regional strategies for teacher in-service education, and initiatives such as those supported by the Open Estonia Foundation, among others, provide excellent beginning points.

- Explore the feasibility of developing an Estonia-wide competency-based general secondary education curriculum at the gymnasium level to be delivered using the Internet and a combination of local technology and traditional instructional materials and support. The goal would be to ensure access to the highest quality curriculum and instruction (especially in certain core areas throughout Estonia and to supplement – but not supplant – the contributions and support of individual local schools and teachers. In a sense, this would be a "virtual Estonian gymnasium". The entity could serve as mentors of pilot testing improvements in the National Curriculum and testing/assessment methodologies to respond to concerns such as the OECD team has mentioned earlier in this chapter. Examples include the importance of addressing the needs of a wider spectrum of student abilities, and more attention to active learning, integration, relationship to real-life and labour market problems.

Note

1. Ene-Margit Tiit and Ants Eglon, Children and education, Children in Estonia, UNDP, 1999, p. 1.

2. European Commission, Eurydice, Supplement to the Study on the Structures of the Education and Initial Training Systems in the European Union, May 1999. The text of this section on pre-school education draws extensively on the Eurydice report, pp. 16-18.

3. European Commission, Eurydice, Supplement to the Study on the Structures of the Education and Initial Training Systems in the European Union, May 1999. The text describing the basic and secondary schools draws extensively on the Eurydice report. pp. 18-23.

4. Eurydice, pp. 8-9.

5. Ene-Margit Tiit and Ants Eglon, Children and education, Children in Estonia, UNDP, 1999, p. 1.

6. Eurydice, p. 18.

7. Ministry of Education, Strategy Platform, 2000-2004, Short Survey, Spring 2000, summary compiled by: Heli Aru, Counsellor to the Minister, and translated from Estonian, 30 March 2000.

8. Statistical Office of Estonia, Haridus 1998/99, table 2.1, p. 30.

9. Statistical Office of Estonia, Haridus 1998/99, table 2.4, p. 34.

10. Eurydice, p. 22.

11. Statistical Office of Estonia, Haridus 1998/99, table 2.6, p. 37.

12. Statistical Office of Estonia, Haridus 1998/99, table 2.5, p. 35.

13. Statistical Office of Estonia, Haridus 1998/99, table 2.30 and 2.31, pp. 62-63.

14. Statistical Office of Estonia, Haridus 1998/99, table 3.7, p. 109.

15. Ministry of Education, draft document on teachers.

16. Statistical Office of Estonia, Haridus 1998/99, Diagrammes 6.1 and 6.2, pp. 224-225.

17. Statistical Office of Estonia, Haridus 1998/99, table 2.4, p. 34.

18. Children in Estonia, UNDP, 1999.

19. Eurydice, p. 19.

20. This section draws extensively from the section by Ene-Margit Tiit and Ants Eglon, Children and education, in the UNDP Report on Children in Estonia.

21. Ene-Silva Sarv, 1999. Teacher Education In a Post-modern Society: An Estonian Perspective. Political And Social Transformations: An Analysis In National Context, Tallinn University of Educational Sciences, 1999, p. 4. This discussion of the evolution of education renewal in Estonia draws extensively on this paper by Ene-Silva Sarv.

22. Sarv, p. 12.

23. Open Estonia Foundation, 1994 Annual Report.

24. Open Estonia Foundation, 1995 Annual Report.

25. Open Estonia Foundation, 1996, 1997 and 1998 Annual Reports.

26. Open Estonia Foundation, 1998 Annual Report.

27. President of the Republic of Estonia, Academic Council, A Learning Estonia, report to the Riigikogu, Tartu/Tallinn, February 19, 1998.

28. K. Loogma, R, Ruubel, Viive Ruus, E, Sarv, and R. Vilu, Estonia's Education Scenarios 2015, Tallinn, 1998, pp. 5-6.

29. K. Loogma, R, Ruubel, Viive Ruus, E, Sarv, and R. Vilu, Estonia's Education Scenarios 2015, Tallinn, 1998, pp. 21-24.

30. Sarv, p. 6 and 13.

31. Minister of Education, Tõnis Lukas, Memorandum to Schools, February 2000 The full text of the draft regulations, the Framework Requirements for Teacher Training, was in the early stages of development at the time of the OECD review.

32. Ministry of Education, statement of priorities and policy directions for reform of teacher in-service training, Tallinn, 1999-2000.

33. Ministry of Education, Estonian Academic Recognition Centre, Higher Education in Estonia, 2nd edition, Tallinn, Draft April 2000, p. 15.

34. Sarv., pp. 5-6.

35. Mart Laanpere, TPÜ Kasvatusteaduste teaduskond, 26.novembril 1998.

36. United Nations Development Program, The Estonian Tiger Leap into the XXIst Century, Tallin, 1998. The sections of this report on the history of ICT in Estonia are drawn largely from the UNDP report.

37. UNDP, Poverty Reduction In Estonia Background And Guidelines, Chapter 4, Tallin, 1999.

38. UNDP 1999 Report, p. 73.

39. UNDP 1999 Report, p. 74.

40. Statistical Office of Estonia, Haridus 1998/99, tables 2.39 and 2.40, and diagram 2.11, pp. 67-68.

41. Open Estonia Foundation Annual Reports, 1996, 1997, and 1998.

42. Ministry of Education, Strategy Platform, 2000-2004, Short Survey, Spring 2000, summary compiled by: Heli Aru, Counsellor to the Minister and translated from Estonian, 30 March 2000.

Chapter 4

Vocational Education and Training

Introduction

As in other parts of the education system, vocational education and training in Estonia have seen substantial change since the restoration of independence in 1991, in response to the ideological changes and the massive labour market dislocations that have occurred. The transition from the previous highly centralised system linked to different sectors of the command economy has been especially difficult. Estonia recognises the need for further changes in order to build the capacity to train the workforce necessary to compete in the global economy. From the perspective of the OECD team, the contrast between the vision of "Learning Estonia" and the reality of the conditions in vocational education and training is stark. The reform of vocational schools was regarded as an urgent necessity by virtually everyone whom the review team met, from the Minister of Education down.

Description of the system

Legal Framework

The Law on Education adopted in 1992 provides the overarching framework for all subsequent laws. In 1993, the process to revise and update laws and policies regarding vocational education and training began. Also, two laws with direct implications for vocational education and training and adult education were adopted. The 1993 Law on Adult Education, subsequently amended in 1998, provides for educational leave for employees, grants for in-service training of teachers and civil servants (no less than 3% of their annual salary fund). Through the 1998 amendments, the Law on Adult Education authorises the National Council on Adult Education. The Law on Social Protection of the Unemployed (1994) sets forth the conditions for training of the registered unemployed.

The first Law on Vocational Education Institutions was adopted in June 1995. In November 1997, discussions began on a possible change to the 1995 law. The proposed amendments were intended to ensure integrated funding of vocational education and training, along with more flexible, transparent programme development and implementation for all interested parties. An important aspect of the reform of the vocational education and training system was the establishment of the National Examination and Qualification Centre in January 1997. This Centre deals with programme development and requirements, qualifications, examinations, assessment and evaluation. In recent years, different interests in society, including employers and local authorities have begun to feel the need to co-operate. The Curriculum Service, initially the Department's third unit, became part of the National Examination and Qualification Centre (*Riiklik Eksami- ja Kvalifikatsioonikeskus*) in 1997.[1]

In January 1998, a "concept document" on vocational education was formally adopted. This set out the principles on which vocational education should be based, including such criteria as efficiency, flexibility, functionality, co-operation, quality and availability. This was followed by the adoption of laws elaborating and clarifying the roles of important elements of the system:

• The Law on Vocational Education Institutions (1998).

• The Law on Applied Higher Education Institutions (1998).

• The Law on Private Schools (June 1998).

The Law on Vocational Education Institutions as amended is intended to ensure integrated financing of the vocational education and training institutions and make the development and application of programmes more flexible. The law specifies the concept and meaning of "secondary vocational education" (*kutsekeskharidus*) and provides guidelines for the provision of "vocational higher education" (*kutsekõrgharidus*). The Law establishes "vocational councils" that are bodies, established at the Estonian Chamber of Commerce and Industry, consisting primarily of the representatives of the social partners, *i.e.* enterprises, trade unions and field specialists. These councils are to deal with the preparatory stage of programme development including qualification requirements and vocational standards to serve as the basis for developing study programmes at educational institutions. At the time of the OECD review, the further elaboration of the status and roles of the vocational councils was still in process.

The amended Law on Vocational Education Institutions also provided for the transfer of the vocational institutions under the Ministry of Agriculture to the Ministry of Education as of 1 September 2000.

Policy structure

As described in Chapter 2, the MoE is responsible for the whole area of education, in particular: administration, approval of admissions, system development and planning, national curricula development, approval of school courses of study and programmes, inspection of schools, supervision of final certificate issue and the organisation of research work. The MoE was restructured in the beginning of 1996 and the Vocational Education and Training department reestablished. Until 1997, the Department had three structural units – Educational Management Service, Curriculum Service and Adult Educational Service. As indicated above, the Curriculum Service function was assumed by the National Exam and Qualification Centre (*Riiklik Eksami ja Kvalifikatsioonikes-kus*).

All ministries and other authorities responsible for vocational education and training institutions act independently of the MoE in supervision and management of vocational schools under their jurisdiction, but they have to follow national education policy as established by the MoE. Principal decisions are drafted and approved by the MoE whose regulations also govern the registration and approval of all study courses. Alongside the vocational education and training reform, there is a clearly organised sharing of interests and responsibilities among national and local authorities. Some local municipalities have already demonstrated interest and initiative by taking part in the reorganisation of the vocational education and training system. At the time of the OECD review, however, there was no consensus on either how to begin the decentralisation process or the legislation required. Municipalities are currently obliged to coordinate and approve admission plans and programmes, but further active participation in the development of vocational education and training is still under consideration.

Under the current system of vocational education, institutions which offer vocational programmes fall under several ministries, municipalities and private organisations, for example: MoE (69 schools, including 13 agricultural schools), National Police Board (1), Ministry of Social Affairs (1), municipalities (3) and private organisations (15). Labour market training is organised by the Labour Market Board and the regional Employment Offices. The training is purchased from different training providers. [2]

Adult and continuing training is provided on a small scale through vocational schools, which provide updating training or training for a specific employer. Vocational colleges specialising in a particular industry also exist. For unemployed people some training or retraining, again on a small scale, is done under the auspices of the Labour Market Board, which reports to the Ministry of Social

Affairs. This training is contracted to vocational schools or, increasingly, to private providers.

Vocational Education and Training System [3]

The changes in 1998 reflect a fundamental redefinition of both vocational education after basic school and post-secondary vocational education. As discussed below, these changes are having significant effects on the roles of schools and institutions throughout Estonia. Until 1998, there were two distinct curricula in the vocational education and training system, established by the June 1995 Vocational Education Institutions Law. Students could enter a VET institution (*Kutseõppeasutus*) after either basic school (*Põhikool*) or general upper secondary school (*Gümnaasium*). Students entering after basic school could obtain a vocational school certificate (*kutseõppeasutuse lõputunnistus*) following 2-3 years of study equivalent to International Standard Classification for Education (ISCED) level 3 /3C, and a post-secondary level qualification (*kutseõppeasutuse lõputunnistus keskerihariduse omandamise kohta*) after four years (ISCED 5/3A). These four-year qualifications were mostly in the fields of art and music. General upper-secondary school-leavers could also enter the same programmes, but get through them more quickly, completing the *kutseõppeasutuse lõputunnistus* in 1-2 years (ISCED 3/4B), and the post-secondary qualifications (*kutseõppeasutuse lõputunnistus keskerihariduse omandamise kohta*) sometimes in as little as two-and-a-half years (ISCED 5/5B). In certain fields, young people entering vocational education after basic school were able to complete additional hours of general upper secondary education (ISCED 3/3A). On passing the state exams, these students receive the same qualifications as those who actually attended school entirely at this level, thus becoming eligible to apply for universities (*Ülikool*) or institutions of applied higher education (*Rakenduskõrgkool*). Students who followed this path received both the vocational and general upper secondary school certificates (*kutseõppeasutuse lõputunnistus kutse- ja keskhariduse omandamise kohta*).

Since approval of the June 1998 Vocational Education Institutions Law, the situation has changed. This new law states that there are two levels in the vocational education and training system – vocational secondary education (*kutsekeskharidus*) and vocational higher education (*kutsekõrgharidus*).

Secondary vocational education

Admission to vocational secondary education may follow either basic education or general upper secondary education. The period of study for those who have left basic school is at least three years (ISCED 3/3B) leading to a secondary vocational education certificate, the lõputunnistus põhihariduse baasil kutse-keskhariduse omandamise kohta. A critical change is that directly after basic school students will no longer be able to obtain the highly specialised vocational training lasting less than three years that was a key mission of vocational schools in Soviet times and up to the 1998 changes.

The reforms in the Estonian education system are leading to a closer relationship between upper secondary general and vocational education and to increased coherence in the requirements for all secondary-level students. In broad terms, the intent is to increase the general education content of the vocational education curriculum and, in time, to increase the opportunities for practical application for students in general secondary education. The plan in the vocational education system is to leave the general education subjects at the same volume, but there is an emphasis on tying the teaching of general subjects with speciality subjects. In this respect, the National Curriculum (see Chapter 3) is the framework for all secondary education and this curriculum is elaborated – especially at the school level – to meet the specific needs of vocational education. The secondary vocational education curriculum now aims to encourage development of the knowledge, skills, experience and attitudes required to perform independent skilled work, on the assumption that trainees have sufficient general education and ability to apply this know-how in both large and small firms after they have qualified. The minimum period of study entailed is 120 weeks, during which the vocational or occupation-related dimension must account for at least 50%.

Since 1997 it is compulsory for secondary school (whether general or vocational) students to pass the state examinations (*riigieksamid*) administered by the National Examination and Qualification Centre (*Riiklik Eksami-ja Kvalifikatsioonikeskus*) to obtain a secondary education qualification.

At the time of the OECD review, the implementation of these changes in vocational education changes was in its early stages. More progress had been made on the changes in curriculum related to general secondary education than on vocational education.. It should be noted that in developing curricula there is a need for co-operation with social partners, and this is a priority for the MoE. However, renewal of specialty teaching should be tied to subject teaching.

Post-secondary vocational education at the secondary level

With respect to further training after completing general secondary education, young people with the general upper secondary school certificate may enter a secondary vocational school and complete the requirements for a secondary vocational education certificate in less time (one or two years corresponding to

ISCED 3/4B). The aim of the revised requirements is to foster the development of expertise, experience and attitudes needed to carry out more complex independent skilled work. The assumption is that these students have already acquired a satisfactory general upper secondary background, along with the ability to grasp technological processes and analysis. In this case, the period of study is a minimum 40-100 weeks, during which the vocational or occupation-related dimension must account for at least 50%. These students are awarded a post-secondary vocational education certificate – *lõputunnistus keskhariduse baasil kutsekeskhariduse omandamise kohta*. In some sectors (such as healthcare and the police) satisfactory completion of general upper secondary education is the prerequisite for entry to vocational education (ISCED 3/4B).

Students who have completed secondary education (whether general or vocational) are eligible for vocational higher schools (ISCED 5B). Those students with a secondary vocational education certificate, who wish to continue their studies in a university (ISCED 6/5A) have to pass the corresponding state exams, similar to those required for students to obtain the general secondary certificate.[4] Since 1997 it is compulsory for secondary school (whether general or) students to pas the state examinations (riigieksamid) administered by the National Examination and Qualification Centre (*Riiklik Eksami-ja Kvalifikatsioonikeskus*).

Distinction between higher schools and higher education

An important distinction is between higher vocational school leading to a secondary-level diploma in a speciality, and the newly refined and higher level of diplom now available within higher education.[5]

- Vocational higher school is a one-stage higher education offered by secondary education based vocational education institutions or rakendus-kõrgkool: (institution of applied higher education. The length of study is three to four years and the total capacity of studies is 120 to 160 credits (180 to 240 ECTS credits). The vocational higher education study programme includes practical training accounting for at least 35%. Vocational higher education study is possible in applied higher institutions and in vocational education schools. Graduates who have completed their studies will be awarded a diploma with indication of the speciality. Generally, the fields of study offered under vocational higher school programmes are nursing, midwifery, social work and social sciences. A graduate from vocational higher education has the right to continue academic studies, according to the university board's requirements.

- Diplom-study is a one-stage non-academic applied higher education leading to a diplom-study diploma. The length of study and the capacity of studies are similar to the vocational higher education curriculum 120 to 160 credits (180 to 240 ECTS credits), but the proportion devoted to acquiring practical knowledge and skills is lower (no less than 10 credits or 15 ECTS credits). The graduates are also awarded a *diplom*. *Diplom-study* can be either at university or rakenduskõrgkool. The study programme of *diplom-study* at university may have a common part with bakalaureus-study.[6] Graduates from diploma studies have the right to continue academic studies, according to the conditions posed by the university board.

- The MoE plans in the near future to standardise the conditions in applied higher education, abandon diploma studies. A common vocational higher education will be developed.

These changes can be difficult to understand from the international perspective, especially because of the ambiguities during a period of transition. The effects of the new requirements are to both increase the general content and requirements for vocational higher schools as well as raise the requirements to obtain a diplom to a level appropriate for designation as "higher education." As illustrated above, the distinctions are somewhat blurred in practice. A number of vocational schools, which teach according to vocational higher education curricula, offer both study programmes leading to a secondary-level vocational education certificate and vocational higher education "diplom".

Institutions and schools/institutional network and study programmes

There were approximately 90 vocational education institutions in Estonia in 1998/99. As indicated above, the ambiguity arises in the period of transition from the 1998 policy changes and the change in institutional classification from vocational education institutions to institutions of applied higher education. The 1997/98 edition of Haridus, the compilation of education data by the Statistical Office of Estonia, includes the following note:

> "A number of vocational educational institutions have lately developed into professional higher schools, but at the same time some of them continue to give vocational education as well. Data about those can be found under both corresponding levels. Compared with last year [1996]…the decrease [in enrolment] at professional secondary education is connected with the transfer of some medical programmes to the higher level category."[7]

129

Table 16. **Number of vocational education institutions
and number of students in 1992/93 - 1998/99**

Year		Ministry of Education	Ministry of Agriculture	Other (incl. Private)	Total
1992/93	# of Schools	45.0	12.0	30.0	87
	# of Students	19 527.0	3 677.0	7 486.0	30 690
	% of Total	63.6	12.0	24.4	100
1993/94	# of Schools	63.0	12.0	8.0	83
	# of Students	24 302.0	3 257.0	649.0	28 208
	% of Total	86.2	11.5	2.3	100
1994/95	# of Schools	63.0	13.0	11.0	87
	# of Students	22 684.0	2 708.0	2 414.0	27 806
	% of Total	81.6	9.7	8.7	100
1995/96	# of Schools	59.0	13.0	13.0	85
	# of Students	24 444.0	3 084.0	1 9109.0	29 438
	% of Total	83.0	10.5	6.5	100
1996/97	# of Schools	60.0	13.0	18.0	91
	# of Students	24 924.0	3 374.0	3 189.0	31 487
	% of Total	79.2	10.7	10.1	100
1997/98	# of Schools	58.0	13.0	18.0	89
	# of Students	24 846.0	3 513.0	2 957.0	31 316
	% of Total	79.3	11.2	9.4	100
1998/99	# of Schools	56.0	13.0	20.0	89
	# of Students	25 012.0	3 483.0	2 695.0	31 190
	% of Total	80.2	11.2	8.6	100

Source: European Training Foundation, Estonian National Observatory, Vocationall Education And Training System, March 1999, p. 40; Ministry of Education,Information and Statistics division.

The statistical report for 1998/99 cites 87 vocational education institutions, but includes the following note reflecting the fluidity of the situation as institutions adjust to the new requirements and economic conditions.

"The number of listed institutions is 87 (of which 13 are private), including 1 professional higher school (kõrgkool), 4 study centres (õppeskust) and 1 general education school (üldhariduskool). In addition, graduates of 6 institutions have been shown (2 vocational education institutions were closed, 2 general secondary schools closed the vocational programmes, 1 vocational education institution was joined with another and 1 music school is no longer considered as a vocational education institution)".[8]

Table 16 provides an overview of the numbers of schools and students in the period from 1992/93 to 1998/99. As indicated by the foregoing notes, the recent decrease in schools and enrolments may reflect reclassification as much as actual changes. Nevertheless, the changes illustrate the underlying trend away from traditional vocational schools and toward schools at the "higher professional school" level or applied higher education.

Seven state vocational education institutions offer vocational higher education programmes according to the Law on Vocational Educational Institutions and may also offer vocational higher education. These include Kohtla Järve Meditsiinikool (Kohtla Järve Medical School), Tallinna Kergetööstustehnikum (Tallinn Technical School of Light Industry), Tallinna Majanduskool (Tallinn School of Economics), Tallinna Meditsiinikool (Tallinn Medical School), Tallinna Pedagoogiline Seminar (Tallinn Pedagogical Seminary) and Rakvere Pedagoogikakool (Rakvere Pedagogical School). These institutions may offer also vocational education, which is not part of higher education.[9]

As might be expected, approximately half of the schools and most vocational education enrolments are concentrated in Tallinn, Tartu, and the other larger population centres such as Kohtla-Järve, Pärnu, and Narva. This concentration is reflected in Figure 12 showing the origin of new entrants. Of the schools located in these five cities, 73% had total enrolments in 1998/99 were greater than 400 and 13% had enrolments greater than 700. The schools in small towns and elsewhere in Estonia are smaller and more highly specialised. The 13 schools under the Ministry of Agriculture are all far from the larger population centres. Of the institutions in smaller towns and rural areas, only 14% have enrolments greater than 400 and 21% enrol fewer than 200 students. Not only the size and complexity of the urban schools are different, but also the students they service. The urban schools generally serve large numbers of evening and correspondence students, whereas the schools in other areas of Estonia tend to serve traditional daytime students.[10]

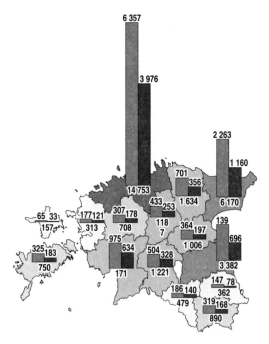

Figure 12. Number of students enrolled in vocational schools by counties (1 October 1999), Graduates in the end of 1998/99 and admission in 1999/00 academic years.

Source : Estonian National Observatory, 1999. Key : Light grey=entrants, Grey=graduates.

Student attendance patterns

Student choice reflects a decline in the number of students entering vocational education directly following basic school – or, expressed differently, a distinct preference for students to enrol in upper-secondary general education (*gümnaasium*). The most precipitous decline occurred shortly after independence. From 1991 to 1997, the proportion of those completing basic education who entered vocational education (kutseõppeasutused) fell from over 43.8% in 1991 to 26% in 1997.[11] It may however be misleading to compare the two dates, since in 1991 the Soviet industrial structure was still in place and vocational education may have seemed a reasonably attractive option. But there can be no doubt of the relative popularity of the gymnasium compared to the vocational stream today. 70% of those going on to upper secondary education after basic school chose gymnasiums in 1997 and 1998.[12] Information received by the OECD review team indicates that the fields of specialisation offered in vocational education and training institutions may not be attractive to the young, while the period of training is a long one. According to application forms received from young people, vocational education and training seems to be the least popular among the study opportunities available from age 16 onwards – a fact that significantly influences the quality of learning activity. At the same time, however, interest in vocational education and training has increased among those successfully completing upper secondary education.[13]

The Vocational Education Concept set forth a target of achieving parity between gymnasiums and upper secondary vocational education institutions, with 50% of the basic school graduates enrolling in each and 50% of the age group of the graduates of basic school enrolling in applied higher education.[14] At the moment this target looks to be out of reach unless the current problems of vocational schools are resolved.

The changes in distribution of enrolments across different educational levels since 1992/3 are shown in Table 17. While enrolments in vocational education increased, this occurred at the upper secondary level and not in traditional vocational education programmes (ISCED 3/3C).

As described below, the policy direction since the mid-1990s has been to strengthen the relationships between vocational education and general secondary education. The MoE's current policy objective is to increase the general curriculum requirements for secondary vocational education and increase the opportunities for practical application (*e.g.*, apprenticeships) for general secondary (gymnasium) students.[15]

Language of instruction

In about 60% of the 90 or so institutions which provide vocational education and training Estonian is the sole language of instruction. Twenty per cent use only Russian, while the others use both languages. By the law, all gymnasium schools will have to move to Estonian as the sole language of instruction after 2007, and if this were to apply to vocational schools it could create transitional problems for them.

Table 17. **Enrolments and students per class by ISCED Level, 1996/97 - 1998/99**

	Enrolments		
	1996/97	1997/98	1998/99
General upper secondary (ISCED 3/3A)	37 532	38 319	37 381
Vocational education total	29 953	30 233	30 264
Vocational education based on basic education (ISCED 3/3C)	1 750	1 793	1 437
Vocational education with upper secondary general education (ISCED 3/3A)	11 519	12 238	12 793
Post-secondary technical education based on basic education (ISCED 5/3A)	4 438	4 231	3 740
Vocational education based on upper secondary education (ISCED 3/4B)	3 288	3 449	4 231
Post-secondary technical education based on upper secondary education (now applied higher education) (ISCED 5/5B)	8 958	8 522	8 063
	Students per class		
General upper secondary (ISCED 3/3A)	27.6*	28.3*	25.8*
Vocational education total			
Vocational education based on basic education (ISCED 3/3C)	24.3	22.9	18.9
Vocational education with upper secondary general education (ISCED 3/3A)	22.2	23.2	23.1
Post-secondary technical based on basic education (ISCED 5/3A)	22.2	20.6	21.25
Vocational education based on upper secondary education (ISCED 3/4B)	24.4	26.7	22.9
Post-secondary technical education based on upper secondary education (ISCED 5/5B)	24.3	23.9	22.6

* Special education is excluded.
Source: European Commission, Eurydice, Supplement to the Study on the Structures of the Education and Initial Training Systems in the European Union, May 1999, p. 25-26.

Table 18. **Vocational education graduates by field during 1997/98**

ISCED Code	TOTAL	Total graduates 1997/98
	Vocational education	5 670
14	Teacher training	22
18	Fine and applied arts	14
34	commercial and business administration	732
46	Mathematics and computer sciences	11
50	Medicine and public health	153
52	Trade, craft and industrial programmes	2 909
54	Engineering	0
62	Agriculture, forestry' and fishery	171
66	Domestic science	292
70	Transport and communication service	66
78	Trades	884
89	Other	416
	Professional secondary education	2 867
14	Teacher training	106
18	Fine and applied arts	169
22	Humanities	8
34	Commercial and business administration	855
38	Law and jurisprudence	166
46	Mathematics and computer sciences	20
50	Medicine and public health	281
52	Trade, craft and industrial programmes	170
54	Engineering	403
58	Architecture and town planning	6
62	Agriculture. forestry and fishery	323
66	Domestic science	30
70	Transport and communication	43
78	Service trades	165
84	Mass communications and documentation	61
89	Other	61

Source: Statistical Office of Estonia, Haridus, 1998/99, Table 4.30, p. 160-161.

Fields of study

Table 18 shows the graduates in academic year 1997/98 by field of study. Most (51%) of the graduates at the vocational education level were in trade,

Table 19. Most popular specialities among new entrants to vocational education, 1997/98 and 1998/99

Speciality 1997/98	Applications	New entrants	Applications per entrant	Specialities 1998/99	Applications	New entrants	Applications per entrant
Vocational education							
Cook, baker	225	106	2.12	Cook, baker	68	32	2.13
Restaurant cook	140	68	2.06	Postal worker	60	34	1.76
Cosmetology	184	54	3.41	Photographer	111	32	3.47
Cosmetology Man/pedicure	119	55	2.16	Data processing and comp networks	81	29	2.79
Court secretary	111	33	3.36	Court Secretary	108	32	3.38
Furniture restorer	81	16	5.06	Furniture restorer	49	23	2.13
Hotel attendant	80	41	1.95	Hotel attendant	180	101	1.78
Cook, pastry (restaurant)	75	36	2.08	Hair dresser	397	204	1.95
Computer network attendant	38	10	3.80	Trade by internet	38	16	2.38
Clerk	27	13	2.08	Information service worker	32	17	1.88
Professional secondary education							
Tourism arrangement	270	94	2.87	Tourism arrangement	366	137	2.67
Hotel and catering manager	323	93	3.47	Hotel management	55	21	2.62
Finances and credit	180	54	3.33	Banking	78	28	2.79
Computers and networks	128	38	3.37	Artistic designing	84	33	2.55
Law (in customs)	105	34	3.09	Optometrist	79	23	3.43
Ballet dancer	99	23	4.30	Ballet dancer	59	21	2.81
Business management (industry)	93	29	3.21	Secretary, travel consultant	148	57	2.6
Popular music	56	17	3.29	Dental mechanics	94	12	7.83
Computer graphics	40	10	4.0	Computer graphics	65	10	6.5
Singing	40	13	3.08	Singing	37	14	2.64

Source: Statistical Office of Estonia, Haridus 1997/98, Table 4.29, p. 156 and 1998/99, Table 4.29, p. 158.

craft and industrial programmes, and another 16% were in fields classified as "trades". Students graduating from commercial and business administration fields constituted 13% of all vocational education graduates. As a reflection of the changing economy, the largest proportion of graduates (30%) at the professional secondary level were from commercial and business administration programmes, followed by engineering (14%) and agriculture, forestry and fishery (11%).

The most popular specialities in 1997/98 and 1998/99 of students entering vocational education are shown in Table 19. While the categories that the Statistical Office uses to report these data differ between the two years, there is a clear difference in the two years. The new entrants in 1998/99 reflected a clearer demand for specialities related to the developing economy (tourism, business and management, information technology, and legal specialities) compared to 1997/98. Whether this difference reflects a trend is not possible to determine from two years' data.

Financing

At the time of the OECD review, the policies regarding financing vocational education were under review. Historically, the State has financed wages and benefits as for basic and secondary general education and the founding ministry or other sponsor has been primarily responsible for other costs (*e.g.*, textbooks, equipment, and maintenance). In principle, vocational education institutions are authorised to generate additional income by undertaking short-term training for adults or other activities financed by business and industry or contracting to provide training for the registered unemployed. The state allocation to each school has been based on a formula including input variables such as the characteristics of student programmes, curriculum, time, and state-defined parameters on the number of required teaching positions. Public vocational institutions have generally been under centralised financial management and control by the sponsoring ministry with only limited authority at the school level.

Now financing mechanisms are to change from a tight control on the basis of normative input criteria towards a financing system according to which lump sums are paid per student. The Ministry of Finance document, "Development Plan for Estonian Economy 1998-2002," approved by the Government in December 1998, establishes the goal of a single purpose complementary training fund for financing a continuous learning system. The intention is to shift away from subsidising institutions and towards a competitive, market-driven system in which State funding would be allocated on the basis of students for priority labour market needs. The system would decentralise management responsibility to the institutional level in order to increase responsibility and accountability for responding to local and regional labour market needs. The historic tight central control would be changed to provide schools with lump-sum payments per capita. The policy would result in substantially increased local responsibility to optimise resource utilisation – meaning in several cases, merger, and consolidation – if not closure – of inefficient, non-competitive schools and programmes.[16]

Issues and observations

The issues identified by the OECD are well known within Estonia at all levels, and the review team heard them from a wide number of sources. Interestingly, they are problems shared by many OECD countries to some degree, though in transition economies they are bound to be more severe because of the huge structural changes in the economies and the desire for very rapid and fundamental reform.

Quality and efficiency of the school network

The need to improve the quality and efficiency of the vocational education and training network is a central concern of all stakeholders. In spite of the progress over the past decade, many schools are too small. The Vocational Education Concept emphasised an optimal school size of 500 minimun, yet more than three-quarters of the schools outside major cities have fewer than 400 students and many have fewer than 200 students. Schools remain highly specialised despite efforts to change and diversify study programmes to respond to the changing economy. In several regions of Estonia, the economy remains severely depressed and vocational schools are often disconnected from efforts to revitalise the regional economy and labour market. With teachers who have not been retrained, outdated facilities and low status traditionally accorded vocational education, the schools have limited capacity to attract and serve students seeking the knowledge and skills to be competitive in the new economy. Under-utilised out-dated facilities add to costs.

In Chapter 3 on general education, the OECD review team underscored the plight of small largely rural basic and upper secondary schools, especially in terms of the capacity of these schools to implement the new, higher expectations of the National Curriculum and testing and assessment requirements. Those same concerns are applicable to vocational schools. Unless the system is restructured to become more efficient, the school network will be unable to meet higher expectations for quality, responsiveness and performance.

The system inherited from Soviet times of highly centralised management and financing linked to different sectors of the economy is a serious barrier the development of a more efficient and responsive system. The historic vertical management structures provide no capacity at the school level to achieve efficiencies. In contrast to the vertical structures of the past, effective vocational and training systems in the future need highly flexible responsive horizontal relationships with:

- Other vocational education and training possibilities serving the same region yet linked by vertical management structures to other sectors of the economy,

- Regional economic strategies,

- Employers,

- General education,

- Municipalities,

- Regional labour market strategies, especially the retraining of the adult workforce,

- Applied higher education and other educational institutions.

Estonian leaders clearly recognise these issues and are committed to address them despite the obvious political issues when subjects such as merger, consolidation and closure of schools are raised. The OECD review team believes that the current strategies of the MoE to address these problems are in the right direction and are consistent with the most progressive actions in OECD countries. The MoE strategic directions include:

- Continued consolidation of the administration of educational institutions.

- Developing regional training centres that become district centres providing primary training for students, retraining for adults, pre-training (opportunities for practical training) for students in general secondary education, and vocational education and training for people with special needs. In 2000, plans call for the opening of vocational training centres as regional development centres in Tallinn, Tartu, Ida-Virumaa and Jõgeva counties. By 2003, the development of regional vocational training centres in Võru, Viljandi and Valga counties should be completed.

- Removing administration of public vocational schools from the MoE and decentralising administrative responsibility to local vocational education and training districts. Foundations would be established to represent state interests and be responsible for the administration of the districts. Instead of retaining centralised management and fiscal controls, the MoE will move to a broader guiding and supervising role in the regulation of the academic process recognising that the state remains the owner of public vocational schools.

- Continuing to implement financing reforms moving toward allocations based on student numbers, lump-sum allocations, and decentralised management responsibility and incentives for developing stronger links with social partners, regional economic development, and optimising resource utilisation – teachers, equipment and facilities.[17]

Decentralisation of the vocational education and training system is a desirable objective. Although Estonia is a comparatively small country, there are significant regional differences in prosperity, economic and industrial structure, and this suggests that there is a case for vocational education and training to be decentralised, within the framework of national policy laid down by the Government. This would have several potential advantages and could engage enterprises more closely with vocational education and training institutions in their localities. In particular, links between schools and employers, so crucial for the successful transition of young people from school to work, would be easier to forge. Local labour market information could be more useful in helping to plan adult and continuing education, if only for relatively short-term needs.

The review team emphasises, however, that, from the experience in OECD countries, the success of the decentralisation will depend fundamentally on two points:

- The capacity of district organisations, regional training centres or other entities to which administrative responsibility is to be delegated – time and resources must be invested in training to develop the necessary management, educational leadership and analytic skills. Resources will be essential to provide the basic infrastructure (*e.g.*, access to information technology). Data and analytic skills will be essential for the entities to analyse and remain responsive to the labour market.

- Accountability mechanisms to ensure that the decentralised system is responsive to both regional needs as well as national (state) policies and priorities.

The OECD team also senses that Estonia's success in implementing a more decentralised, regional vocational education and training system will depend on the development and implementation of basic public administration reforms – especially related to the roles of municipalities and counties. As mentioned below, improved co-ordination across ministries as they affect regional labour market, social welfare and economic policies will also be important.

Teachers and teaching

The quality of teaching in vocational education was widely criticised in the course of the OECD review. Renewing human resources is perhaps the core challenge in reform within the vocational education and training system. Many countries have introduced educational reforms without the necessary work in preparing the front-line teachers on which the success of the reforms depend. Estonia must ensure that it does not make this mistake. The review team is convinced that the MoE clearly recognises this challenge.

It was emphasised that teachers are poorly paid, and it is difficult to attract young graduates to enter the vocational school system. As a result, the teaching workforce tends to be relatively old, with long service in the schools as shown in Table 20 which compounds the problem of inappropriate training. Teachers for the most part have been trained in the Soviet period, and their experience is relevant to teaching for occupations that may no longer exist and in ways that

Table 20. **Vocational teachers - Age, gender, length of service, 1998/99**

		Gender and Age Female			Gender and Age Male		Length of Service	
			Under	Over		Under	Over	0 - 5	> 15
		30	49		30	49	years	years	
Vocational	Number	Number	Per-vent	Per-cent	Number	Per-cent	Per-cent	Per-cent	Per-cent
Teachers									
Full-time									
and	2539	2013	9.1%	32.9%	825	11.6%	44.8%	23.7%	51.7%
Part-time									

Source: Statistical Office of Estonia, Haridus 1998/99, Tables 6.3, 6.6, and 6.8, pp. 228-239.

are out of date in pedagogical terms. The reorientation of the teaching strength is therefore a major priority.[18]

With a staff/student ratio of 1:5, vocational education and training institutions are currently overstaffed and inefficient. One aim of reform is to increase this ratio from around 1:12 to 1:16. The average ratio of teachers to other personnel is only slightly over one, indicating that overstaffing is attributable to the large number of non-teaching staff or to the limited economies of scale in small schools or schools functioning under capacity.

There is currently no institution with an up-to-date teaching methodology for vocational teachers' and trainers' training. Courses are overly academic, focus on general subject matter, and lack the integration of theory and practice. There is little exposure of student teachers to in-company practice and teacher training, and vocational teacher training in particular, were held in low esteem by a number of those seen by the review team.

A MoE Regulation in December 1998 set out new requirements for vocational teachers. They either have to have pedagogic higher education and two years of speciality work experience in the subject to be taught or higher education in the technical field in which they teach and pedagogical training. They also are obliged to spend a two-month practice within a relevant company every three years.

The OECD team strongly supports the MoE policy direction to introduce mentors' training in order to increase the efficiency of the training of the pedagogical personnel and the in-service apprenticeship of the students of vocational educational establishments. Mentor's training would mean that those workers and employees of enterprises who will be supervising trainee teachers and students' apprenticeships in the enterprises will be prepared. In order to provide schools with well-trained vocational teachers the Ministry of Education intends to cover the tuition expenses in foreign countries for teachers seeking training in specialities not available in Estonia.

A particular concern expressed to the OECD team was the retraining of teachers already within the system. Most of these teachers were trained in specific occupations and are usually subject specialists, with little training in teaching as such, so that they are not necessarily professionally qualified to communicate effectively what they know. Furthermore, many teachers are unfamiliar with contemporary technology and teaching methods, in which theoretical, lecture-based courses are giving way to more practical interactive work (including seminars, case studies and independent projects). As a result, they need additional training in order to update their skills. Many of the issues raised in Chapter 3 regarding the need for reorientation of teaching and the preparation of teachers in general secondary education are also directly relevant to vocational education.

As described earlier, the 1993 Adult Education Law provides that a minimum 3% of the salary fund be used for in-service training. Teachers also need regular in-service training in firms – the best way of learning about practical aspects of the workplace and labour market requirements at any given time and a further reason why the education sector should establish closer co-operation with industry and other interest groups in society.

Again, the MoE recognises the severity of the problems and places high priority on retraining of current teachers and school managers. The OECD team strongly supports this position.

The paradox is that this more intensive training may not seem to potential recruits to be balanced by appropriate pay once they are in the profession. The pay differential between the private and public sectors for good teachers with knowledge of the modern skills is very large. An important executive of Eesti Telecom told the review team that a college teacher with skills relevant to their business could earn more than three times as much in private enterprise. It may of course be possible to use more private sector people to work part-time, which is to some extent happening already, and which would help bring modern industrial practice into the vocational education and training system.

Responsiveness to changing labour market and labour market information

The OECD review team was told that the training provided in vocational education is often not related to the future requirements of employers or the Estonian economy. The content of training is often obsolete since many jobs no longer exist in trades. This is a matter partly of poor or non-existent labour market information, but it also reflects the real difficulty in turning round any training organisation to teach new skills. Equipment, facilities, curricula all have to be redirected, and this takes time, money and management skills.

Under the Soviet system, labour market information was irrelevant since the central planning system decided the employment requirements of state enterprises, and vocational education and training was geared to the short-term requirements of enterprises in a given locality. In a market economy, the planning and operation of vocational education and training require a flow of good and timely information on labour market prospects, and the skills likely to be in demand.

This information is ideally needed at several levels. Basic questions are these:

- What is likely to be the broad picture of the country's economic and industrial progress? This does not mean long term manpower forecasting, which is not possible, but rather the perception by industrialists, policy makers and the research community of where the country's comparative advantage lies, and what are likely to be areas of employment growth and decline.

- What are likely to be the changes in skill requirements within existing enterprises and in the new sectors which might act as guidance to the outputs of vocational education and training establishments?

- Are there links between employers and vocational education and training institutions at local level with a regular dialogue about skill needs?

Through the Estonia 2010 Scenarios and the Estonia's Education Scenarios 2015, Estonia stands out in comparison to many other countries in its effort to address the first two questions. The implications of the global economy and information technology have been widely discussed among the nation's leaders as reflected, for example, in the Tiger Leap initiative discussed in Chapter 3 and in reports of the United Nations Development Programme (UNDP).[20] What is lacking, however, is the translation of this excellent forward thinking into concrete information that is useful to those developing the future of the vocational education and training system.

The review team found few people who were content with the current state of labour market information for the vocational education sector. Analysis of the forward prospect for employment is a new and undeveloped area. Though the Labour Market Board is beginning to carry out more analysis, it has a small staff and much of the information is difficult to access. At the local level, labour offices do not have the resources to analyse their labour markets. The Chamber of Commerce has done some work on potential growth sectors, including tourism, food processing (where there is, however, strong competition), and forestry and wood products. The Confederation of Employers and Industry suggested to the review team that possible areas for expansion included microelectronics, marine technology, biotechnology where a good research base exists, and machine tools. Individual employers, especially small and medium sized enterprises, may have little idea of their future skill needs except in very general terms, especially since most firms are relatively new.

There is a clear need to place a higher priority on labour market information at every level of the system, and to strengthen inter-ministerial co-ordination in the collection and analysis of data. It is also important to bridge the apparent gap between the strategic thinking and the practical application in developing a vocational and training system attuned to the dramatic changes taking place in the global economy.

Curriculum and Occupational Standards

In moving from the centralised Soviet system to a more appropriate design, the approach to the curriculum is a flexible, module-based, employer led model. The Chamber of Commerce and Industry, with the agreement of the Ministries of Education and Social Affairs, is in the lead in developing occupational profiles for industrial sectors. The work is being done through tripartite Vocational Councils, with studies of human resource and skill needs within the sectors. The first five sectors to be covered by Vocational Councils are finance and business services, social and health care, retail and wholesale trade, wood processing and construction. The definition of occupation/job profiles was initially difficult, since no reclassification of occupations had been carried out before vocational education and training reform began. Nor is it clear how many occupational profiles will emerge from the Vocational Councils.

The current position is that modular based curricula with test specifications for new courses using a nationally approved industry standard have been developed for 13 occupational groupings for testing in pilot schools. The general approach is to build a unit credit system that is output based with tests after each module. The courses within the vocational programmes are composed of modules to allow for maximum flexibility, easy access and progression towards further qualifications. This type of approach has many advantages: the units are small and more easily understood; training times may be shorter; modules can be tailored to different performance levels; and modules can be adapted more quickly to labour market or company requirements.

Notwithstanding these merits of flexibility, implementation of this kind of system is not without its problems. These may include the relative isolation of modules which, without an overall approach to their structure, could result in lack of coherence. For example, trends in Europe and elsewhere suggest that, while there is a universal need by employers for higher-level cognitive and social/behavioural skills, the number of occupations can be reduced by combining several profiles. In addition, the very flexibility and adaptability of modules can bring its own problems. Unrestricted expansion of the numbers and varieties of modules could bring confusion to employers, individuals entering vocational education and training and to the system as a whole. Finally, the temptation to shorten initial training periods must not be allowed to develop into narrow track training, which could have negative consequences for further progression and for lifelong learning.

Another issue concerns the relationship between the specific curriculum development around modules and the curriculum development associated with the National Curriculum for basic and secondary education as discussed in Chapter 3. The National Curriculum is intended as a framework for both general education and vocational education; elaboration of the specific curricula is to take place within that framework. In Chapter 3, the OECD team expressed concerns that the National Curriculum currently is highly subject oriented and gives inadequate attention to integration of subject matter and practical application. A strongly subject oriented curriculum, targeted at the needs of students who intend to pursue further academic study, will not provide for adequate integration with vocational curricula, and will be inappropriate for students intending to enter the labour market or further training in vocational fields.

The OECD review team generally agrees with the approach of Estonia to curriculum reform, but would make three recommendations. First, while the OECD team lauds the goals and philosophy underlying the National Curriculum for basic and secondary education, the team urges the MoE to revise the detailed implementation of that curriculum to ensure that they support the development of an appropriate curriculum for vocational education. These issues are discussed in greater detail in Chapter 3. Secondly, to avoid excessive diversification, a national resource centre should co-ordinate module design and the process of review. This centre would act as a central point of advice and materials for vocational education and training establishments. Thirdly, the experience of the pilot schools should be cascaded, with training and the full involvement of the original course designers, to other schools. The MoE has already expressed its intent to utilise pilot schools as centres for the development of vocational training within the framework of the vocational education reform as a priority in its draft Strategy Platform for 2000-2004.[21]

Examination and certification

The current system of assessment in vocational education and training institutions is unsatisfactory. Those completing courses are given a certificate, but this does not represent a formal qualification but simply attests to attendance at a course and the grade achieved on a five-point scale. It is acknowledged that development of a new system of qualifications is very important. The National Centre for Examinations and Qualifications will presumably take the lead. The Centre is in charge of national curricula, assessment and examinations, and will in effect be the accreditation body in respect to vocational education and training qualifications. The initial step was to consider the module descriptors for the pilot schools for accreditation and approval, so as to test out the link between the content of courses and the qualification structure.

Progress in this area seems to have been rather slow, and yet the establishment of a widely accepted qualifications system is very important in assuring individuals of the value of their study and employers of the usefulness of the training. It should also facilitate progression, enabling people to deepen and upgrade previously acquired competencies. The OECD review team believes that the qualifications verified in the certification system should be based on national skill and knowledge standards. They should cover all levels of vocational education and training, ranging from the basic vocational qualification which might be appropriate for someone with no educational qualifications, through the courses run for unemployed people, to the higher level skills which are likely to be in demand by employers. The certification system should also be able to cope with learning pursued in a variety of ways – work experience, training in the workplace, and completion of courses in vocational education and training establishments. Finally, the issue of cross-border recognition of qualifications is important in the context of future accession to the EU and the need then to ensure that there are no barriers to free movement of labour. The Estonian system will have to ensure transparency and comparability with EU standards.

The OECD team is also concerned, as expressed in Chapter 3, that the system of assessment and testing for basic and secondary education may not give adequate attention to the knowledge and skills needed by all students – but especially for students pursuing vocational education and training. The OECD team urges Estonia to recognise the need for state exams that are appropriate for the students at all ability levels as well as those for whom a less-discipline/subject matter orientation would be more appropriate.

Students within the system

Access to vocational education and training places, which are assured for all who opt for this educational path is of great importance. Students can apply for different programmes and institutions at the same time, which can create confusion since there is no national record of applications and places accepted. As noted earlier, a condition of entry to vocational education is the completion of basic education, and this obviously works against the least able students. Labour market prospects are poorest for the least skilled and it might seem appropriate that some low-level vocational skills should be offered to those with the poorest education, so as to give them a somewhat better chance of employment.

147

Apart from this, and the relatively poor image and unpopularity of vocational schools, two other points emerged during the review team's discussion. First, counselling and guidance services are inadequate, and there has been recognition by both the MoE and the Ministry of Social Affairs that career advice, placement and follow-up are needed. The old system with careers advisers in each school was abolished in 1993, and the responsibility now lies with individual schools and counties whether they consider this area sufficiently important to warrant scarce resources. Helpfully, a database is now available on the Internet of learning opportunities at secondary schools, higher education establishments and qualifications that can be acquired. This however will be most useful for those who have a clear view of their own abilities and who know pretty well what they want to study. Advice and counselling require a different approach.

Secondly, Estonia appears to be facing a growing problem of dropouts who leave the education system with insufficient training to be successful in the labour market over the long term. As discussed in Chapter 3, the number of adolescents without a basic education (grade 9) is increasing. The highest dropout rate is among boys in grades 8 and 9 (15% in Estonian schools and 9% in Russian schools). Among the girls, the highest rate of dropouts is in the 10th grade (7% in Estonian and 5% in Russians schools).[22]

The changes made as a result of the 1998 Law on Vocational Education Institutions now require that students entering vocational secondary education following basic school complete a minimum of 3 years of training. No longer can students enter vocational school for shorter periods of training for specialised positions as was possible before the new law and especially in Soviet times. The general education dimensions of the curriculum are now more extensive and rigorous. While the OECD team applauds the strengthening of vocational secondary education, the question remains about how Estonia is addressing the needs of those students who drop out of school before completing basic school. The team understands that vocational schools still serve these students if they return to school. The MoE plans soon to open groups in vocational education schools for pupils without basic education.

A broader problem – also discussed in Chapter 3 – is that the National Curriculum for basic and secondary education and the national assessment and examination policies set exceptionally high expectations and, in the view of many interviewed by the team, focus on those students at the highest ability levels. Several prominent Estonian leaders expressed concerns that education reforms were giving inadequate attention to the "average" student. The OECD team urges Estonia to ensure that the secondary education system - including both general and vocational education – provide sufficient diversity to serve students in the full range of ability levels.

Adult and continuing education and training

Training provision for adults is through the Labour Market Board for unemployed people, and through vocational schools, colleges and private training providers. For the unemployed, labour market training is one of the active policy measures aimed at getting people back to work. This can involve adaptation courses on job seeking skills, refresher courses for those who already have some skill, or retraining courses for those requiring new skills. While these courses are useful, it is generally recognised that they are quite inadequate to deal with the needs of the unemployed.

First, the courses are only available to the registered and, as Chapter 1 pointed out, about half the unemployed do not register. The courses are also not available to those facing future unemployment. Secondly, there are too few training places to cope with the demand even for the registered unemployed. The review team was told that unemployed people are becoming more interested in training. In Tartu there are 1 000 training places for 6 000 registered unemployed, with at least twice as many applicants as places. Thirdly, the budgets of local labour offices are very limited in terms of the overall amount and the flexibility with which money can be spent. Given that training courses have tended to become more expensive, this further limits the number of trainees.

Private providers under contract carry out most of the training offered by labour offices. This avoids the inflexibility often found in vocational schools and colleges, and since many of the providers are new, they may be able to offer more up-to-date training. In addition the labour office can set conditions under the contract, for example that a certain proportion of trainees should find jobs afterwards. In Tartu the placing rate was 75% and the national rate is apparently similar. This is a creditable performance even if most training is short-term.

The Law on Vocational Education Institutions permits vocational schools to offer training to adults, and most do. As pointed out earlier in the discussion of institutions and student enrolments, only the schools in Tallinn and Tartu and other major cities appear to serve a significant number of students through means that are usually appropriate for adult learners – evening and correspondence programmes. Few institutions provide training at or in conjunction with the workplace and, therefore, they are likely to be inappropriate or inaccessible to adults seeking to upgrade their current skills.

149

There is no formal policy towards adult or continuing training, and no data to show how extensive it is, how it is financed and how successful it is in terms of quality. It does appear, however, that there is a great deal of activity in this area. One estimate is that there are more than 900 providers in the sector, and that the participation rate in continuing education and training in 1997 was about 25%. A study of small and medium enterprises suggested that most trainees had attended courses organised by private companies [23] which suggests that many such courses will be closely geared to business needs.

There is, however, a clear gap in national policy here. Other sectors of education are clearly important, but the lack of a strategy towards adult and continuing training – and by implication towards lifelong learning – is extremely serious given the likelihood of continuing structural change in the Estonian economy and labour market and the need for the redeployment of the workforce. With a declining school-age population, Estonia must continue to depend on its current adult population for its workforce over the next decade and beyond. While the education level of adults is generally high in Estonia, the adult population needs access to retraining to gain the knowledge and skills for the new economy. Increasing the knowledge and skills of that population should be a central national priority and a core mission of the vocational education and training system. Language training is an important dimension of the national strategy, but specific knowledge and skills for the labour market are also important. The developing network of regional training centres will be an important means to address this problem.

Strategy and its implementation

The Estonian system of vocational education and training is in the process of reform at all levels. This section picks out four areas which, in the opinion of the OECD review team, need particular attention and which have a bearing on the efficiency of the system. There has been a great deal of debate within Estonia about the strategy for reform, and the concept of vocational education and training. This is to be welcomed since without a clear strategic view, reforms may be piecemeal and poorly co-ordinated. There appears to be a high degree of political consensus on the direction of reform that again is essential. The review team would note a number of points about this process and the follow-up.

Co-ordination across ministries

It is essential that Government Departments work closely together in the development of strategy and, even more, in the policy formulation that follows. The MoE has quite rightly been in the lead on educational reform, with the

Ministry of Social Affairs taking a back seat: it had a major job in coping with the unemployment that followed independence. But especially in vocational education and training, it is crucial that there is a common view and understanding between these Ministries, and the Ministry of Economy, about the future shape of the Estonian economy, the pattern of different areas of reform – the labour market, the economy, and education. This common view and understanding should include the implications of these developments for the vocational education and training sector, including adult and continuing training.

Social partners

As in most transition economies, it has proved difficult to get a full engagement of social partners. The employers' associations are developing a useful role, especially in the construction of the vocational qualifications system, but the small and medium sized firms which are the growth sector in Estonian employment may not be sufficiently represented. Trade unions are very weak, with a role still to find in the process of educational reform. It is important to have a much fuller involvement of the social partners, since there has to be social as well as political consensus on reform, and a full understanding and acceptance of the many difficult policy decisions that have to be taken. This means a clear definition of the social partners' roles, including their future role in the context of EU accession, and the adoption of policies by Government to build up their capacity to fulfil their expected roles.

System integration

The vocational education and training system needs to be seen as an integrated whole, and must be designed to meet the needs of all citizens. At the moment, the system seems to fall short of these aims. The different parts of the system tend to have policies developed separately from on another and in some important areas such as adult and continuing training there is a real shortage of reliable information. Obviously there have to be priorities for the implementation of reform, but policy development – not only strategy – should be pursued across a broad front, which will in any case be necessary if lifelong learning is to become a reality. The review team was impressed by and wholly agrees with, the observation by the Minister of Education that the main task was to raise the average quality of education. It would be all too easy to concentrate on highly technical and advanced skills in the vocational education and training system, but the national strategy, including much greater access to the disadvantaged, will best be achieved through improving the overall level of efficiency throughout the system.

Recommendations

The OECD team supports the basic policy directions of the MoE to improve the quality and efficiency of vocational education and training in Estonia. The team believes that these policy directions are sound and consistent with the serious challenges facing Estonia and the most progressive developments in OECD countries. The following recommendations are intended to reinforce these directions:

- Establish a stronger link between the strategic thinking of initiatives such as Estonia 2010 Scenarios, the Estonia's Education Scenarios 2015, and "Learning Estonia," as enunciated by the President's Academic Council, and strategies for the future of vocational education training.

- Bridge the strategic thinking and the practical application in developing a vocational and training system attuned to the dramatic changes taking place in the global economy.

- Pursue the goal of a more integrated vocational education and training system designed to meet the needs of all citizens. Such a system should counter the current fragmentation among critical elements of the system. Pursue policy development – not only strategy – across a broad front aimed at a lifelong learning system for all Estonia.

- Build upon the strong foundation of the growing consensus around the vision of "Learning Estonia," and place a high priority on translating this vision into concrete policy implementation. Give greater attention to narrowing the gap between the realities of the current vocational education and training and adult and continuing training systems in Estonia and the promise of the vision of "Learning Estonia".

- Place the highest priority on the renewal of human resources within the vocational education and training system.

- Continue to pursue the recently approved increased requirements regarding the qualifications of teachers within the vocational education and training system.

- Continue to pursue the initiative to introduce mentors' training in order to increase the efficiency of the training of the pedagogical personnel and the in-service apprenticeship of the students of vocational educational establishments.

- Continue to give high priority to the retraining of the current teachers and school managers.

Recognise that any initiatives to improve the quality of vocational education and training system must give priority to:

- Ensuring much greater access – especially to special needs populations, regions that continue suffer several economic and social dislocation and all people regardless of language or ethnicity.

- Improving the overall level of efficiency throughout the system.

Continue efforts to improve the quality and efficiency of the vocational education and training system by pursuing policies of:

- Consolidating the administration of educational institutions.

- Developing regional training centres that provide primary training for students, retraining for adults, pre-training (opportunities for practical training) for students in general secondary education, and vocational education and training for people with special needs.

- Removing administration of public vocational schools from the MoE and decentralising administrative responsibility to local vocational education and training districts.

- Continuing to implement the financing reforms moving toward allocations based on student, lump-sum allocations, and decentralised management responsibility and incentives for developing stronger links with social partners, regional economic development,and optimising resource utilisation – teachers, equipment, facilities.

Provide essential support for developing the local capacity for the decentralisation of vocational education and training by investing in:

- Train the necessary management, educational leadership, and analytic skills.

- Develop the basic infrastructure (*e.g.*, access to information technology).

- Develop the data and analytic skills will be essential for local entities to analyse and remain responsive to the labour market.

- Develop an accountability system to ensure that the decentralised system is responsive to regional needs as well as national (state) policies and priorities.

- Recognise the importance to education reform of basic public administration reforms especially related to the roles of municipalities and counties – and of improved co-ordination across ministries as they affect regional labour market, social welfare and economic policies.

- Place a higher priority on Labour Market information at every level of the system, and strengthen inter-ministerial co-ordination in the collection and analysis of data.

- Continue to pursue curriculum reform in a manner consistent with the vision of "Learning Estonia" and the principles that under-pin the new National Curriculum for basic and secondary education the process of revising the National Curriculum.

- Ensure that the curriculum is appropriate for students in the full range of abilities and for those who intend to pursue vocational education.

- Give more attention to curricular elements that support integration of subject matter and pedagogy, integration of practical application with theory, and other curricular dimensions that are important for reach all students, but especially students in vocational education and training.

- Continue to pursue development of curriculum modules in vocational education and training. Consider establishing a national resource centre to co-ordinate module design and the process of review as a means to avoid excessive diversification in the vocational education curriculum.

- Utilise pilot schools as centres for the development of vocational training within the framework of the vocational education reform.

Give higher priority to the establishment of a widely accepted qualifications system, which is very important in assuring individuals of the value of their study and employers of the usefulness of the training. Such a system should:

- Facilitate progression, enabling people to deepen and upgrade previously acquired competencies.

- Allow for the qualifications verified in the certification system to be based on national skill and knowledge standards.

- Cover all levels of vocational education and training, ranging from the basic vocational qualification which might be appropriate for someone with no educational qualifications, through the courses run for unemployed people to the higher level skills which are likely to be in demand by employers.

- Provide for the certification of learning pursued in a variety of ways – work experience, training in the workplace, and completion of courses in vocational education and training establishments.

- Be designed to ensure cross-border recognition of qualifications in the context of future accession to the EU and the need to ensure that there are no barriers to free movement of labour.

- Ensure transparency and comparability with EU standards.

- Recognise the need for state exams that are appropriate for the students at all ability levels as well as those for whom a less-discipline/subject matter would be more appropriate. Ensure that the system of assessment and testing for basic and secondary education pays adequate attention to the knowledge and skills needed by all students – but especially for students pursuing vocational education and training.

- Strengthen counselling and guidance services throughout Estonia (perhaps on the base of the newly developing regional training centres). Emphasis through both the MoE and the Ministry of Social Affairs that career advice, placement and follow-up are needed for both youth and adults in all regions of Estonia.

- Focus attention on alternatives to address the growing problem of school dropouts. Recognise that the strategies should include developing a more diversified secondary education system (including curriculum and assessments) appropriate to serve students from the full range of ability levels – especially the "average" student.

- Establish a national strategy for adult and continuing training in recognition of the critical need to prepare Estonia's adult population for the likely continuing structural change in the Estonian economy and labour market in the global economy.

155

- Seek greater involvement of the social partners in the education reforms to ensure that there is a deeper social as well as political consensus on reform, and a fuller understanding and acceptance of the many difficult policy decisions that have to be taken.

- Seek a clearer definition of the social partners' roles, including their future role in the context of EU accession.

- As necessary, adopt governmental policies to build up the capacity of social partners to fulfil their expected roles (*e.g.*, tax policies).

Notes

1. European Commission, Eurydice, Supplement to the Study on the Structures of the Education and Initial Training Systems in the European Union, May 1999, pp. 23.

2. European Training Foundation, Estonian National Observatory, National VET System, Revised March 1999. p. 40.

3. European Commission, Eurydice, Supplement to the Study on the Structures of the Education and Initial Training Systems in the European Union, May 1999, p. 24.

4. European Commission, Eurydice, Supplement to the Study on the Structures of the Education and Initial Training Systems in the European Union, May 1999, p. 24. This description of the vocational education system draws extensively on the Eurydice report.

5. The term "professional" is used in lieu of "vocational" in many of the translations from Estonian for the designations of vocational institutions at the upper-secondary "higher school".

6. Ministry of Education, Estonian Academic Recognition Information Centre, Higher Education in Estonia, Second edition, Tallinn, draft April 2000, p. 19.

7. Statistical Office of Estonia, Haridus 1997/98, p. 16.

8. Statistical Office of Estonia, Haridus 1998/99, p. 178.

9. Ministry of Education, Estonian Academic Recognition Information Centre, Higher Education in Estonia, Second edition, Tallinn, draft April 2000, p. 11.

10. Statistical Office of Estonia, Haridus 1998/99, Table 4.37, p. 172-178.

11. European Commission, Eurydice, Supplement to the Study on the Structures of the Education and Initial Training Systems in the European Union, May 1999, p 23.

12. Ministry of Education, Information and Statistics Division; European Training Foundation, Estonian National Observatory, National VET System, Revised March 1999. p. 23.

13. European Commission, Eurydice, Supplement to the Study on the Structures of the Education and Initial Training Systems in the European Union, May 1999, pp. 23.

14. Vocational Education Concept, as referenced by European Training Foundation, Estonian National Observatory, National VET System, March 1999, p. 23.

15. Ministry of Education, Strategy Platform, 2000-2004, Short Survey, Spring 2000, summary compiled by: Heli Aru Counsellor to the Minister and translated from Estonian, 30 March 2000.

16. European Training Foundation, Estonian National Observatory, National VET System, March 1999, p. 46.

17. Ministry of Education, Strategy Platform, 2000-2004, Short Survey, Spring 2000, summary compiled by: Heli Aru Counsellor to the Minister and translated from Estonian, 30 March 2000.

18. European Commission, Eurydice, Supplement to the Study on the Structures of the Education and Initial Training Systems in the European Union, May 1999, pp. 25-26.

19. Ministry of Education, Strategy Platform, 2000-2004, Short Survey, Spring 2000, summary compiled by: Heli Aru Counsellor to the Minister and translated from Estonian, 30 March 2000.

20. See Loogma, R, Ruubel, Viive Ruus, E, Sarv, and R. Vilu, Estonia's Education Scenarios 2015 , Tallinn, 1998, UNDP Report, 1999, and UNDP, The Estonian Tiger Leap Into the XXIst Century. Tallinn, 1998.

21. Ministry of Education, Strategy Platform, 2000-2004, Short Survey, Spring 2000, summary compiled by: Heli Aru Counsellor to the Minister and translated from Estonian, 30 March 2000.

22. Ene-Margit Tiit and Ants Eglon, Children and education, UNDP Report on Children in Estonia, Tallinn, 1999.

23. Raul Eamets and Kaia Philips, Estonian Labour Market and Labour Policy, Country Study presented to ILO, Tartu, 1998.

Chapter 5

Higher Education

Higher education in Estonia has undergone fundamental changes since the late 1980s – in mission, the relationship of institutions to the government, content and structure of curriculum and degree programmes, financing, and many other areas. After a period of dramatic change in which virtually every dimension of the system was changed in the early 1990s, Estonia is now in the process of making reforms in financing, quality assurance, and the institutional network to accommodate escalating demand.

Overview of the Estonian higher education system [1]

Legal basis

Laws governing the system include:

- Law on Universities (January 1995),

- Law on the University of Tartu (January 1995),

- Law on the Organisation of Research and Developmental Activity (April 1997).

- Law on Private Schools (June 1998),

- Law on Applied Higher Education Institutions (June 1998), the Law on Vocational Education Institutions (July 1998).

The Standard of Higher Education (*Kõrgharidusstandard*) of 1996 specifies requirements to higher education in Estonia and is a fundamental act for granting education licences and for accreditation of study programmes or higher education institutions. The Standard of Higher Education is based on other acts related with higher education and is valid for all stages or forms of higher education irrespective of owners or legal status of higher education institutions. The MoE is responsible determining whether institutions meet the requirements of the Standard of Higher Education.

Leadership and responsible entities

Responsibilities of the MoE regarding higher education policy include:

- Regulating the establishment, merger, partition or closure of universities on the basis of decisions made by the *Riigikogu* (Parliament), and of applied higher education institutions on the basis of decisions made by the Government.

- Keeping the registry of recognised final documents issued by universities and applied higher education institutions.

- Approving, discussing, and forwarding the budgets of universities and distributing budgeted funds to the applied higher education institutions.

- Approving the development plans of universities and of applied higher education institutions.

- Adopting the procedures for the opening and closing of study fields and specialities.

- Carrying out State supervisory activities.

Public universities (Ülikool) are autonomous under the administrative jurisdiction of the MoE. The autonomy ensures universities the right to independently determine :

- The academic and organisational structure,

- The content of the teaching and research work,

- The organisation of teaching,

- The course curricula,

- The conditions for admission and graduation, the organisation of research work, and

- The employment terms for teaching staff and researchers and the selection of candidates.

The MoE is assisted in its role by a number of management and consultative bodies with an administrative or teaching function:

- Higher Education Advisory Chamber (*Kõrghariduse Nõukoda*), a consultative body of representatives of higher education institutions at the MoE dealing with the problems related to higher education institutions.

- Estonian Research and Development Council (*Eesti Teadus- ja Arendusnõukogu*), a consultative body in the Government chaired by the Prime Minister.

- Estonian Science Foundation (*Eesti Teadusfond*), a consultative body of experts, representatives of universities and of the MoE deciding on financing the science projects.

- Higher Education Quality Assurance Council (*Kõrghariduse Hindamise Nõukogu*), a body responsible for the accreditation of the higher education institutions and study programmes.[2]

The Archimedes Foundation is an independent unit under the MoE responsible for organising and managing the activities of different aid and co-operation programmes of the European Union. In addition, Archimedes plays an important role as the organisation home of the Higher Education Quality Assessment Centre. Units within the Foundation include:

- Phare programmes including Higher Education and Science Reform, Information Systems in Education (a project aimed at developing the use of ICT in school management carried out in collaboration with Tiger Leap, as described in Chapter 3), and the Phare Multi-Country Distance Education Programme.

- EU Co-operation Programmes, including Youth for Europe and Socrates (ERASMUS and COMENIUS), among others.

- Estonian Programmes, including the Higher Education Quality Assessment Centre (responsible for institutional and study programme accreditation), and the national contact point for the EU RTD Fifth Framework Programme.

- EU information projects.

System structure [3]

As a result of the laws enacted in the mid-1990s, Higher education in Estonia is now divided into:

- Universities (*Ülikoolid*), which offer the following academic higher education and diploma programmes:

- Diploma programmes involving 3-4 years of study, ISCED 6/5A, (*Diplomiõp*).

- Bachelor's courses entailing 3-4 years of study, ISCED 6/5A, (*Bakalaureuseõpe*).

- Master's courses involving 1-2 years of study, ISCED 7/5A, (*Magistriõpe*).

- Doctoral studies entailing four years of study, ISCED 7/6 (*Doktoriõpe*).

Applied higher education institutions (*Rakenduskõrgkoolid*) which offer the following:

- Diploma programmes involving 3-4 years of study, ISCED 6/5A (*Diplomiõpe*) and

- Vocational higher education programmes involving 3-4 years of study, ISCED 5/5B (*Kutsekõrgharidus*).

- Vocational Education and Training Institutions (*Kutseõppeaasutused*) which also offer the *Kutsekõrgharidus*.

Qualification structure

As a result of the Law on Higher Education Institutions, Estonia formally changed from the former Soviet degree structure to one that conforms more closely to Western systems. This structure has recently been further modified to reflect the Bologna Joint Declaration.[4]

Non-academic higher education qualifications

As described in Chapter 4, there are two levels of applied higher education, one level at ISCED 5B and the other at 5A. The length of study is similar for both, but the emphasis on practical training is greater for vocational higher education and these may be awarded by institutions that primarily offer secondary vocational education.

- Vocational higher education is a one-stage higher education programme offered by secondary education based vocational education institutions or *rakenduskõrgkool*. The length of study is from three to four years, the total capacity of studies 120 to 160 credits (180 to 240 ECTS credits). Vocational higher education study programme includes practical training with total capacity of at least 35%. The graduates who have completed their studies will be awarded a diploma with indication of speciality – *Kutsekõrgharidus* (ISCED 5/5B). Generally the fields of study offered by the vocational higher education programmes are nursing, midwifery, social work, pre-school teacher training and social sciences. Vocational higher education study may have a common part with diplom-study at *rakenduskõrgkool*.

- Diplom-study diploma (*Diplomiõpe*). Diplom-study is a one-stage non-academic applied higher education programme. The length of study is from three to four years, the total capacity of studies is 120 to 160 credits (180 to 240 ECTS credits) and consisting of studying and acquiring practical knowledge and skills. The acquirement of practical professional and working skills, including training must have a total capacity of no less than 10 credits (15 ECTS credits). The graduates who have completed their studies will be awarded a Diplomiõpe ISCED 6/5A Diplom-study can be performed at university or at *rakenduskõrgkool*. The study programme of diplom-study at university may have a common part with bakalaureus-study.

Academic Higher Education

- Bachelors degree (*Bakalaureusekraad*). Bakalaureus-level study is the first stage of academic study and serves to increase students level of general education and develop theoretical knowledge and professional skills for the selected area of employment and further study. The length of bakalaureus-level study was four years (reflecting the Bologna Joint Declaration, beginning in 1999, it is now 3 to 4 years) and the maximum of credits is 160 (240 ECTS credits). This is a wide-ranged study based on scientific treatment, research and professional or creative work, including a final thesis which must have a value of no less than 20 credits (30 ECTS credits). Graduates completing their studies receive a diploma, certifying that they obtained the bakalaureusekraad (ISCED 6/5A).

- Masters Degree (*Magistrikraad*). Magister-level study is the second stage of academic study, the main purpose of which is to deepen theoretical and

163

specialist knowledge and develop proficiency in research, professional or other creative work for individual use of knowledge and skills. Admission requirement is the *bakalaureusekraad* or an equivalent level of academic education. The length of study is two years (reflecting the Bologna Joint Declaration, beginning in 1999, it is now 1 to 2 years), but together with the bakalaureus-study, no less than 5 years, with the total capacity of 40-80 credits (60-120 ECTS credits). These changes were due to the Higher Education Standard adopted at the beginning of summer 2000. Studies must be completed with the defence of a thesis that may be of a theoretical or of a professional nature. Research work must take up at least 50% of the research master's study curriculum. The master's thesis must have a novel research approach. The curriculum for a professional master's must contain at least 25% research, development or creative work. The professional master's curriculum contains emphasis on increasing practical skills, resulting in finding new creative solutions to professional problems.

• Graduates who have completed their studies will receive a diploma, certifying that they obtained a *magistrikraad*. (ISCED 7/5A).

• Doctorate (*Doktorikraad*). Doktor-study is the third stage of academic study, consisting of comprehensive research, professional or other creative work and interrelated studies. Admission requirement for doktor-study is the *magistrikraad* or an equivalent level of academic education. The nominal length of study is four years with the total capacity of 160 credits (240 ECTS credits). The *doktorikraad* is divided into research and professional degrees. The study programme for the research degree must include research of no less than 112 credits (150 ECTS credits). The study programme for professional degree must include research, development-oriented or other creative work of no less than 80 credits (120 ECTS credits). Graduates who have completed their studies will receive a diploma, certifying the acquired *doktorikraad*. By the internal regulations of some universities, a Latin version of academic degree may also be used as a state diploma (doctor *philosophiae*, doctor *iuris*, doctor *medicinae* or doctor *theologiae*) (ISCED 7/6).

Degrees in special professional fields

Basic medical study consists of studying and acquiring practical skills. The length of study is six years with the total capacity of 240 credits (360 ECTS credits). Basic medical study is a one-stage academic study and the graduation level corresponds to magister-studies. Graduates who have completed their studies will receive a diploma, certifying the acquired Medical Doctor degree (arsti aste).

Study programmes in the field of Veterinary Medicine, Pharmacy, Stomatology and Architecture (arhitekt-insener-study) take five years with the total capacity of 200 credits (300 ECTS credits). The graduates will receive a diploma with indication of speciality.

Teacher study is performed in the form of diplom-study or passing an additional study programme after bakalaureus or diplom-study at universities or rakenduskõrgkool. The capacity of the additional teacher study programme is 40 credits (60 ECTS credits). At least 25% of the training course must be teaching practice. Graduates who have completed the programme will receive a tunnistus (certificate), certifying programme completion.

Institutions

There are six public universities in Estonia:

- *Eesti Kunstiakadeemia* (Estonian Academy of Arts).

- *Eesti Muusikaakadeemia* (Estonian Academy of Music).

- *Eesti Põllumajandusülikool* (Estonian Agricultural University).

- *Tallinna Pedagoogikaülikool* (Tallinn Pedagogical University, recently renamed the Tallinn University of Educational Sciences).

- *Tallinna Tehnikaülikool* (Tallinn Technical University).

- *Tartu Ülikool* (University of Tartu).

The Estonian system of higher education consists of six private higher education institutions at which at least one study programme is accredited or conditionally accredited by the MoE. Private higher education institutions provide study programmes mainly in the field of Social Sciences (Economics, International Relations, Law), Business Administration or Theology.

- *Audentese Kõrgem Ärikool* (Audentes Business School).

- *Concordia Rahvusvaheline Ülikool Eestis* (Concordia International University Estonia).

- *Eesti Humanitaarinstituut* (The Estonian Institute of Humanities).

- *Eesti Kõrgem Kommertskool* (Estonian Business School).

- *Eraakadeemia Nord* (Private University Nord).

- *Õigusinstituut* (Institute of Law).

Applied higher education institutions (*rakenduskõrgkool*) provide non-academic higher education (*diplom-study*) with emphasis on professional skills and abilities. As described above, the institutions may also offer vocational higher education programmes.

The Estonian system of higher education consists of eight state applied higher education institutions:

- *Eesti Mereakadeemia* (Estonian Maritime Academy),

- *Sisekaitseakadeemia* (Estonian National Defence and Public Service Academy),

- *Kaitseväe Ühendatud Õppeasutused* (Estonian Joint Military Educational Institutions),

- *Tallinna Tehnikakõrgkool* (Tallinn College of Engineering),

- *Tartu Lennukolledž* (Tartu Aviation College),

- *Tartu Õpetajate Seminar* (Tartu Teacher Training College),

- *Viljandi Kultuurikolledž* (Viljandi College of Culture),

- *Virumaa Kõrgkool* (Virumaa College).

The Estonian National Defence and Public Service Academy, and the Estonian Joint Military Educational Institutions (consisting of five colleges) are special higher education institutions under the responsibility of the Ministry of Internal Affairs. The diplomas awarded by those institutions have the same validity as the corresponding higher education diplomas obtained on satisfactory completion of the Diplomiõpe.

Six state vocational education institutions provide vocational higher education programmes according to the Law on Vocational Educational Institutions and may offer diplom-study:

- *Kohtla-Järve Meditsiinikool* (Kohtla-Järve Medical School),

- *Tallinna Kergetööstustehnikum* (Tallinn Technical School of Light Industry),

- *Tallinna Majanduskool* (Tallinn School of Economics),

- *Tallinna Meditsiinikool* (Tallinn Medical School),

- *Tallinna Pedagoogiline Seminar* (Tallinn Pedagogical Seminary),

- *Rakvere Pedagoogikakool* (Rakvere Pedagogical School).

Private higher education institutions are required to have a teaching license from the MoE in order to carry out instruction at the higher education level. Private higher education institutions or their study programmes are officially recognised after accreditation. Private higher education institutions have the right to award a state diploma or degree after accreditation and only to the graduates having completed the accredited study programme. According to the Law on Private Schools (July 1998), qualifications awarded up to two years before the accreditation decision shall be recognised as state diplomas.

There are five private applied higher education institutions at which at least one study programme is accredited or conditionally accredited by the MoE:

- Estonian-American Business College, (*Eesti-Ameerika Ärikolledž*),

- Theological College, (EEKBL *Kõrgem Usuteaduslik Seminar*),

- Theological Institute of the Estonian Evangelical Lutheran Church, (EELK *Usuteaduse Instituut*),

- Baltic Mission Centre Theological Seminary (*Eesti Metodisti Kiriku Teoloogiline Seminar*),

- Mainor School of Economics, (Mainori Majanduskool).

Quality assurance [5]

Accreditation is a process by which an institution, a study programme or a specialised unit of higher education periodically evaluates its educational activities. Through the accrediting process the institution seeks an independent judgement by experts that it achieves its own educational objectives and meets the established standards of the body from which it seeking accreditation.

According to the Law on Universities (1995), all study programmes in universities must be evaluated and accredited once every seven years. This applies also for applied higher education institutions. The accreditation of universities and applied higher education institutions and their study programmes is granted by the Higher Education Quality Assessment Council (*Kõrghariduse Hindamise Nõukogu*) which was established in 1995. The latter is formed by the Government of the Republic and operates under the administrative jurisdiction of the MoE. The Council forms evaluation committees on the recommendations of which the Council makes proposals to the Minister of Education regarding universities or applied higher education institutions and their operation. These committees are made up of representatives of research and development institutions as well as of researchers from two foreign countries. The participation of foreign researchers is intended to guarantee the greater objectivity of the evaluation.

In 1997, the administrative office of Estonian Higher Education Accreditation Centre (*Eesti Kõrghariduse Akrediteerimise Keskus*) was established within the Archimedes Foundation. The centre prepares all relevant documentation for the Higher Education Quality Assessment Council, including self-analysis reports and reports by expert commissions, as well as the main documents for accreditation of study programmes.

Two types of accreditation are available:

• Institutional accreditation: Focused on a higher education institution as a whole or for its structural units, the purpose is to evaluate the institutional organisation and management, the effective use of resources, and the creation of a favourable environment of studies.

• Programmatic accreditation: Focused on individual study program-mes, the purpose: to evaluate the conformity to the Standard of Higher Education, including the level of the applicable theoretical and practical instruction, the research and teaching qualifications of the teaching and research staff. It also serves to evaluate the quality of education received by the students, especially by graduates.

There are three accreditation categories:

• Accredited: Indicates that the higher education institution or the study programme meets the set of requirements. The decision may also include recommendations for eliminating minor shortcomings. Accreditation is valid for seven years from the date of decision.

- Conditionally Accredited: Indicates that an institution or study programme under review has major shortcomings that need to be eliminated or addressed. In this case accreditation will be in force for two years from the date of the decision. At the end of this period the re-accreditation is relevant, but the "Conditionally Accredited" status cannot be renewed.

- Not Accredited: Indicates that the institution or study programme has serious shortcomings that jeopardise the quality of graduates' knowledge and skills.

Upon receipt of a first negative accreditation decision ("Not Accredited"), for an institution or study programme, the university or applied higher education institution may apply for a second accreditation, one year after the first decision. If a second accreditation has not been applied for within three years after a negative accreditation decision or if there is a second negative accreditation decision, then admission of students to the applicable field of study will cease, or it will be closed. If more than 1/3 of the study programmes of a university or applied higher education institution receive a negative accreditation, the education license will be cancelled and the operation of the higher education institution will be terminated. Higher education institutions and their faculties cannot organise studies in disciplines for which they have not been accredited.

Right to award a diploma or degree

Public universities and state applied higher education institutions, rakenduskõrgkoolid and some vocational schools recognised by the state have the right to award applicable diplomas or degrees. Private institutions only have the right to award the applicable diploma after a study programme has been accredited. Private higher education institutions must have a teaching license from the MoE in order to carry out instruction on a higher education level. However, accreditation is not compulsory for the private higher education institutions. Nevertheless, accreditation of study programmes is necessary for them to have state recognition.

Admissions requirements [6]

There are both general and specific requirements providing access to studies at the first stage of higher education. Two general requirements are common for admission to higher education: a secondary school leaving certificate (*gümnaasiumi*

169

lõputunnistus) and a certificate of state/national examinations (*riigieksamitunnistus*) which provides admission to either diploma or Bachelor's courses. As regards the former, secondary education can be obtained, as already discussed, at either upper secondary schools (*gümnaasium*) or at upper-secondary vocational schools from which students will graduate with the *lõputunnistus kutse- ja keskhariduse omandamise kohta* (vocational school certificate). For admission to vocational higher education (*Kutsekõrgharidus*), the secondary vocational education certificate is now required under the two June 1998 Laws on Vocational Education Institutions and Applied Higher Education Institutions respectively, while, for some courses, the requirements are the same as those for diploma or Bachelor's courses. The post-secondary qualification, *lõputunnistus keskerihariduse omandamise kohta* may also be regarded as equivalent to a secondary school leaving certificate.

Specific requirements depend on the higher education institution and area of specialisation. They may relate to the number of examinations, ranging from one to four, their form (written, oral or interview), or other considerations such as the average grade obtained on the secondary education leaving certificate or the grade in a given subject. In public universities, the basis for admission is the enrolment control number (state order) fixed by the State and covered by the State allocation. But universities have the right to take further students who pay for their places over and above this State quota.

Students wishing to continue their studies in Estonia on the strength of a foreign academic certificate, diploma or degree should apply directly for admission, or for recognition of their qualifications, to the higher education studies or ENIC/NARIC programme co-ordinators. Estonia signed and ratified the Council of Europe and UNESCO convention on the recognition of diplomas and qualifications concerning Higher Education in the European Region (Lisbon, 1997).

Language of instruction

While the language of instruction is usually Estonian (for 83.7% of students), an increasing number of courses are given in English (for 3.0%), while some universities provide courses in Russian for the Estonian Russian minority (for 13.7%).

Financing

The State finances public universities and publicly maintained higher education institutions primarily on the basis of a state order for state-funded student places in study programmes. State funding is also provided for student stipends and benefits, some research functions, and other purposes. Institutions are authorised under certain defined conditions to admit students beyond the state-funded places on a fee-paying basis. The State may also fund student places in priority fields at private institutions provided that the study programme is accredited. Study loans are available for all full-time students.

The 1995 Law on Institutions of Higher Education granted universities substantial autonomy in not only academic policy but also fiscal and human resource management. While the policy direction is to decentralise the management of other higher education institutions, they still remain under far more direct financial control of the MoE than the universities. As discussed later in this chapter, the MoE was considering changes in higher education financing policy at the time of the OECD review.

Science policy and research [7]

Estonia has a rich tradition of scientific activities dating back to the XVIIth century. After dramatic changes in the XVIIIth century, the University of Tartu gained an international reputation in the XIXth century. By the XIXth century the importance of knowledge and school was widely accepted by Estonia. In 1991, after Estonia became independent, professors at Taru University started teaching in Estonian and scientific terminology in Estonian was developed. At the same time, scientific research prospered in several fields.

In the 1920s and 1930s Estonian research in astronomy, medicine, geobotany, shale oil and technology gained world-wide recognition. In 1936, Tallinn Technical University was established and became the centre for higher technical education and technical sciences in Estonia. In 1938, the Estonian Academy of Sciences was founded as a body of prominent Estonian scientists, science societies and institutions, conducting fundamental and Estonian-oriented research. By 1939, Estonia possessed the basic research institutions needed for national development. This changed abruptly with World War II and Soviet occupation.

Under Soviet rule, Estonian science organisations were centralised and guided by socialist ideology and attention to national culture and heritage was minimal. Some branches of science, such as the social sciences were given no freedom at all. Despite Soviet control, however, science continued to develop in Estonia, especially the physical and natural sciences.

An important feature of Soviet research policy was the establishment of research institutes outside universities. Graduate education at the doctoral level was carried out primarily at these research institutes and not at universities. While university professors often had research institute appointments, the mission of the university was narrowly defined – most often in terms of preparing professional and technical workers for a specific sector of the economy. The Estonian Academic of Sciences during Soviet times was the entity responsible for the research institutes and for implementing Soviet research policy.

A major restructuring of science in Estonia began in 1988 at the same time as other early movements for education reform. In the period since then, and especially since independence was re-established, the focus has been on restructuring the decision-making process for science in Estonia, reorganising the research establishments and reforming the education system.

In 1997 a new law on the Organisation of Research and Development was adopted. This law defines the roles of the principal governmental institutions and funding bodies. Among other points, the law establishes the Research and Development Council as an advisory body to the government on overall science policy. The Estonian Academy of Sciences in its Soviet form ceased to exist and was reconstituted as an honorary society drawing together the most distinguished researchers from throughout Estonia. The Academy is no longer responsible for research institutes but plays an advisory role in advancing the general level of research and development in Estonia.

Perhaps the most important change in science and research in Estonia has been the re-establishment of research and doctoral level education as a core university mission. While several research institutes remain independent entities, others have been integrated into the universities. The result has been a significant strengthening of the research capacity and intellectual resources of the universities.

Issues and Observations

Progress in reform

Estonia has made great strides in restructuring its higher education system since the major changes began in 1988. Changes emphasised by higher education leaders in the course of the OECD review included:

- Instilling democratic principles and processes throughout the university, including the free election of the rector and academic deans.

- Establishing a new legal framework providing for institutions of higher education, university autonomy, a new research infrastructure, the framework for quality assurance, and a differentiated higher education system.

- Redefining the role of the MoE – moving from rigidly administered state universities subordinated to the MoE to extensive autonomy in academic policy, internal management, salaries and human resource management, and fiscal affairs leading to greater academic innovation and flexibility to respond to market trends.

- Reforming the financing policies to provide lump-sum allocations to universities, explicit recognition of both the teaching and research mission, and elimination of the detailed input line item (salaries, etc.) controls by the MoE.

- Eliminating previous restrictions in content and pedagogy, especially in the social sciences and humanities, and eliminating required military retraining as a compulsory part of the curriculum.

- Broadening the university mission from the narrow focus of Soviet times to now include teaching, research and community service. Recognition of research as a core, integrated mission of the university.

- Diversifying the higher education system from the highly specialised, limited opportunities in Soviet times, to six public universities, eight applied higher education institutions, six private institutions, and several other institutions authorised to offer programmes at the higher education level.

- Carrying out dramatic shifts in academic programmes in response to changing student demands and the economic reality of the need to generate additional revenue from fee-paying students to offset limitations in state funding.

- Developing – with recognition and support by the Government – of the universities as critical national resources for community service and economic development.

- Moving from the narrow Soviet degree structure to an award structure that is not only more flexible but also consistent with Western models and increasing expectations (*e.g.*, Bologna) for common structures across Europe and the world.

- Abolishing the Academy of Sciences as a research organisation, reconstituting the Academy as an honorary society, integrating research into the universities and creating other independent Estonian research centres, resulting in substantial gains in research and greatly strengthened universities.

- Strengthening graduate education, especially through the integration of research and teaching at the doctoral level in contrast to the location of doctoral programmes outside the universities in Soviet times.

- Greatly expanded service mission including services to regions utilising open/distance learning and other means to provide access to higher education, joint research projects, and collaboration with local governments and social partners throughout Estonia.

At the time of the OECD review, there was growing recognition that further changes in higher education policies would be necessary to: accommodate the escalating demand; strengthen alternatives to university higher education; tighten quality assurance requirements; and reform higher education financing. Having gained consensus around the vision of "Learning Estonia", Estonian leaders faced the challenge of shaping concrete strategies to narrow the gap between that vision and current realities. The following are several of the major issues regarding higher education raised in the course of the OECD review.

Major issues

Escalating demand

Estonia is experiencing a surge of demand for higher education and is confronting many of the same issues about capacity, diversification, quality, and financing that other nations face as they move from elite to mass systems. The increased demand for higher education is a world-wide phenomenon – in Latvia, Lithuania and Estonia, in Europe and, especially in developing countries.[8]

Tables 21 and 22 display the principal dimensions of the recent expansion in Estonia.

A growing percentage of secondary school leavers elect to go to programmes recognised as higher education and a smaller proportion is choosing vocational education.

- The pace of increased participation in higher education increased dramatically over the 5-year period from 1994/95 to 1998/99. In 1995/96, 67.7% of secondary general education (Gümnaasium) graduates went on to higher education encompassing the full range of vocational and academic

Table 21. **Further studies of the graduates from the diurnal secondary general school (Gümnaasium) in 1993- 98**

	1993/94	1994/95*	1995/96	1996/97	1997/98	1998/99
Graduates	8 569	6 650.0	8 787.0	9 435.0	9 551.0	9 216.0
Vocational education	8 63.0	780.0	929.0	1 094.0	910.0	1 003.0
%	10.1	11.7	10.6	11.6	9.5	10.9
Post secondary technikal education	1 179.0	995.0	1 485.0	1 804.0	1 449.0	1 198.0
%	13.8	15.0	6.9	19.1	15.2	13.0
Total higher education	3 411.0	2 652.0	3 539.0	4 235.0	5 031.0	5 856.0
%	39.8	39.9	40.3	44.9	52.7	63.5
Diploma studies	990.0	650.0	1 016.0	1 614.0	2 046.0	2 597.0
%	11.6	9.8	11.6	17.1	21.4	28.2
Bachelor studies	2 421.0	2 002.0	2 523.0	2 621.0	2 985.0	3 259.0
%	28.3	30.1	28.7	27.8	31.3	35.4
Total higher education	5453.0	4427.0	5953.0	7 133.0	7 390.0	8 057.0
(including vocational Education)	63.6	66.6	67.7	75.6	77.4	87.4

Source: Ministry of Education. Note: * Smaller number of secondary school graduates in 1994 was a result of the addition of the 12th grade to the school with tuition in Russian.

programmes and 40.3% went on to higher education defined as diploma and bachelors studies. In 1998/99, the percentage going on to all higher education increased to 87.8% and the percentage to diploma and bachelors studies increased to 63.5%.

- Reflecting the higher participation rates, from 1995/96, graduates from secondary general school (*Gümnaasium*) increased from 8 787 to 9 216 or 4.8%. Over the same period, as shown in Table 22, enrolment in the higher education increased from 27 234 to 40 621 or 49%.[1]

- The most significant increase in participation was in diploma programmes – from 11.2% of secondary general education graduates in 1995/96 to 28.2% in 1998/99. Those going on to the bachelors studies also increased but by a slower pace – from 28.7 to 35.4%. Presumably, the slower rate for bachelors studies reflects greater university selectivity and limitations in state-funded places at this level. The increase in diploma programme participation as well as enrolments may also be attributed in part to the new requirement that teachers be educated at the higher education level.

175

Table 22 **Institutions providing higher education and enrolments, 1994/95 to 1998/99**

	1994/95		1995/96		1996/97		1997/98		1998/99		Percent Change 1994/95 to 1998/99
	(1)	(2)	(1)	(2)	(1)	(2)	(1)	(2)	(1)	(2)	(2)
Total	22	25 483	27	27 234	32	30 072	35	34 542	37	40 621	59.4
Full-time		20 050		22 794		25 768		29 032		34 106	70.1
Evening		1 449		1 442		1 881		3 297		3 484	140.4
Correspondence		3 984		2 998		2 423		2 213		3 031	-23.9
Diploma		5 793		6 063		7 772		10 481		14 997	158.9
Bachelors		17 376		17 959		18 770		20 489		21 731	25.1
Masters		1 926		2 588		2 803		2 673		2 822	46.5
Doctorate		388		624		727		899		1 071	176.0
Public universities	6	20 161	6	19 945	6	20 609	6	22 231	6	24 740	22.7
Private universities	-	-	1	949	1	1 219	4	3 291	5	4 561	380.6
Public higher schools	8	2 291	8	2 591	8	2 835	8	3 285	9	3 616	57.8
Private higher schools	8	3 031	11	3 618	12	4 619	13	4 527	13	5 917	95.2
Vocational education institutions	-	-	1	131	5	790	4	1 208	4	1 787	126.4

(1) = Institutions.
(2) = Enrolment.
Source: Statistical Office of Estonia, Haridus 1998/99, Table 5.1,Tallinn 1999, p. 184.

- The proportion of secondary general education graduates electing to go to vocational education declined during the period, especially post-secondary vocational technical education, reflecting a trend discussed in Chapter 4.

Estonia is also evolving a far more diverse higher education system. In just a few years, the system has gone from a principally public system with most of the enrolment concentrated at the public university level, to a system in which private institutions and vocational institutions are enrolling larger proportions of the students. The principal changes reflect the growth of private universities, and the development of other institutions at the vocational "higher school" level both public and private.

- From 1994/95, enrolments in public universities increased 22.7% but the share of total enrolment at the public universities decreased from 79.1% to 60.9%.

- Private universities have grown at an exceptional rate and now constitute an important share of total enrolments. The first private universities were recorded in 1995/96. From that year to 1998/99, private university enrolments increased 380.6% and the share of total enrolments increased to 11.2%.

- Public and private higher school enrolment also increased during the same period, but private schools increased at a faster pace. Public schools essentially maintained their share of total enrolment, but private higher schools in 1998/99 constituted 14.6% of enrolment.

- Vocational schools offering programmes classified as higher education increased enrolment in the period but constitute only a small proportion (4.4%) of total enrolment.

Data on enrolment by degree level (Table 22) show growth at all levels but especially at the diploma level. Diploma level enrolments constituted 33.8% of bachelors enrolment in 1995/96, but increased to 69% of bachelors studies by 1998/99.

Enrolment at the masters degree level increased at a slower pace reflecting, that the demand in the labour market for this level of education has yet to develop in Estonia. The increase at the doctoral level is a result, in part, from the decision to move this level of education from the institutes of the former Soviet-era Academy of Sciences to the university.

In summary, the escalating demand is at all levels of the system, but the data show an intensifying demand at the "middle" level – at ISCED 5A and 5B, and, to an extent, 4B – areas where the Estonian system seems to be especially under-developed. A growing number of private providers are entering the market with programmes that appear to be competing more effectively for the increased demand than the public higher schools and other available public providers.

Strengthening diversification and the non-university sector

Throughout the review the OECD team heard repeated expressions of concern about the escalating demand for higher education and the lack of diversification – in particular, the lack of an effective system to attract and accommodate students at the applied higher education level. One observer predicted there would soon be structural unemployment of university graduates because the supply of graduates from academic higher education was outstripping labour market demand. In Soviet times, the balance between academic and vocational education at the secondary level was 50-50, now it is 30-70, and would be 10-90 if the students could have their way. The MoE, in its recent strategy document, points out that traditionally the proportion of students pursuing academic higher education has been very high in Estonia. The MoE sees danger in conti-nued increases in the proportion of the secondary graduating cohort demanding entrance to academic higher education. [10]

Part of the problem is manifest in the ambiguities regarding the meaning of study programmes and credentials in the "middle-level" between secondary general and vocational education (ISCED 3A/B) and applied and academic higher education (ISCED 5A/5B). What appears to be happening is that there is growing pressure for institutions offering study programmes at the ISCED 4B level to offer programmes at the 5B level. Then, students who complete these program-mes expect that their credentials will be accorded the same standing as a diplo-ma at the ISCED 5A level (either academic or applied higher education). In other words, a growing array of institutions both public and private are offering – or seeking authorisation to offer – " diploma " level higher education study programmes, but the capacity to offer such programmes and the quality vary dramatically. The pressures for this development come from both student demand and the " prestige " associated with higher education compared to voca-tional education.

The impact of escalating demand and the proliferation of providers is put-ting exceptional pressure on Estonia's faculty resources. New providers, espe-cially private institutions, have depended heavily on hiring part-time faculty from the public institutions, taking advantage of the low wages of these faculty in their regular institutional assignment. The pressures are especially intense in high demand areas such as law, business, economics, foreign languages, and information technology/computer science. Public institutions such as the University of Tartu have been able to counter this trend. Since universities are authorised to accept fee-paying students above the student places financed by the State, institutions such as Tartu have taken advantage of the increased enrol-ments (including students served through the Open University) to increase reve-nues to offset limited State funding and to increase faculty salaries and provide other incentives for faculty not to seek employment outside the institution. In addition, faculty must disclose outside employment as part of their contracts with the university. Tartu has also used its flexibility gained through autonomy to pay higher salaries in high-demand fields – a practice that can also create tensions between high-demand and low-demand departments (and, by definition, between the old economy and the new).[11]

Despite the internal strategies of strong institutions such as the University of Tartu, the broader problem of dispersion of limited faculty resources is clearly a major problem facing Estonia. Increasing the number of small institutions, both public and private, aspiring to offer university level programmes, only compounds the problem.

The OECD team learned that Estonia is considering – or in the process of carrying out – several important policy alternatives to address the needs to develop a more clearly differentiated, higher quality institutional network at the non-university level – ISCED 5B. Essentially two strategies are being pursued. First, over the past five years several previously independent higher vocational schools or colleges have been absorbed by one of the universities. For example, the University of Tartu now has three colleges (kolhedzhid) – Narva, Pärnu and Türi. These institutions are organised as integral elements of an expanding, nation-wide regional network, including centres and support services for the Open University (see below). The college in Pärnu offers programmes at diploma (ISCED 5B) level in business administration, social work, hotel management and tourism. Tartu University – Narva College was founded in July 1999 from the former Narva Teacher Training College (Narva higher school – Kõrgkool). As a unit of Tartu University, Narva's mission continues to be to train teachers with a particular emphasis on the needs of the predominantly Russian-speaking population in the region, but will also become a cultural centre for people living in Ida-Viru county and north-east Estonia.

As another example, Tallinn University of Educational Sciences since 1998 has had responsibility for Haapsala College in the Lääne region in north-western Estonia. The college developed out of the former teacher education institutions (Lääne Opetajate Seminar and Haapsula Pedagoodiline). Under the university, the college now has a mission of offering diploma level studies in elementary education. And computer science/information technology, providing services and support to local schools in the region, and serving as a resource centre (especially for ICT).

From the OECD team's perspective drawing on the experience of other countries, linking developing regional colleges to one of the universities has a number of advantages. The colleges gain a level of academic expertise, instructional support, technology and fiscal management that would be difficult to achieve alone. The institutions become important links between the sponsoring university and regions. The colleges can become support centres for students enrolled in open/distance learning programmes, as well as links between local schools and municipalities for in-service training and technical assistance. From a pragmatic perspective, the universities gain the potential for additional revenue (from fee-paying students and other services) and important local and regional political links. From the perspective of the communities, they receive the benefits of the prestige and name of the sponsoring university.

In spite of these positive points, the OECD team cautions that colleges should be insulated to a degree from the strong academic, discipline-oriented culture of the university faculty. Strong colleges offer professional/vocational programmes and should have strong horizontal relationships with employers and the regions they serve. Their curriculum should provide for a high degree of integration of academic subjects and opportunities for practical application. The upward pull of the vertical relationships with the university can undermine the college's mission unless deliberate safeguards are taken to counter this tendency.

Another alternative under development in Estonia is the consolidation, merger or affiliation of several comparatively small, specialised institutions serving the same region to form a larger entity. At the time of the review, several configurations were under consideration for institutions in Tallinn and in the south of Estonia. The Vocational Education Concept adopted in 1998 (see Chapter 4) called for professional/vocational institutions at the higher education level to have a minimum of 1 000 students. From a comparative perspective, the OECD team agrees that, if institutions are to function as independent entities and not be linked to a university, they should be of sufficient size to develop the necessary core academic resources (faculty, instructional resources, information technology, etc.) and economies of scale.

Independent "colleges" have the advantage compared to university controlled institutions of being able to develop the important cultures, curricula, and horizontal relationships with employers and the labour market without the potentially negative "academic" pressures from a university association. Because much of Estonia is comparatively rural, it will be important to develop networks of colleges to ensure that services are available in regions where a large entity would simply not be feasible. Also, even though these institutions may be "independent," strong alliances with the universities should be encouraged. Through open/distance learning (see below), students attending any institution should increasingly be able to gain access to courses and course-modules offered by other Estonian institutions or, for that matter from institutions throughout the Nordic region, Europe and the world.

The OECD strongly supports the current initiatives of the MoE to pursue these and other alternatives to develop a stronger network of "colleges" throughout Estonia. Such a network is essential to meet the growing demands for student access and the nation's future labour market needs. Given the diversity of the country, a combination of institutional approaches is likely to be the most appropriate strategy.

The OECD team recommends, however, that Estonia pay particular attention to the co-ordination among institutions, centres, branches and other entities serving the same municipality or region. Co-ordination will be especially important between higher education institutions in each region and the regional centres for in-service teacher training mentioned in Chapter 3 and the developing regional training centres related to vocational education and training discussed in Chapter 4. The danger is that several different entities in a locality (each affiliated with a different university or network) will compete against each other for students, resources and political support. A degree of competition is important – especially if it is based on competition to provide high quality services. Nevertheless, in an age of open-distance learning and broadening application of ICT, the emphasis should be on collaboration and strategic alliances – to ensure that the people in a given locality get the best available services. For example, a college connected to one of the universities could also be the venue for open/distance learning programmes offered by an independent "polytechnic" college or from another country through a Baltic-Nordic consortium.

The key to developing regional co-ordination and collaboration is most often in the State financing policies. Institutions should receive funding on not only the number of students served but also the extent to which they collaborate with other institutions to ensure that students, employers, or communities receive the highest quality, most cost-effective service. The OECD team recommends that this point be seriously considered in any revision of current financing policy (see below).

The OECD team also supports the efforts of the MoE to strengthen the provisions of the Standard for Higher Education and accreditation requirements. Several of those interviewed in the course of the review stressed that the requirements were inadequate to curb the proliferation of highly questionable providers. As mentioned below, this will be a growing problem as open/distance learning becomes even more of a mode of delivery than it is today. The need for tighter requirements applies to accreditation of both study programmes and institutions. As a basic requirement, no study programme should be accredited unless an institution can demonstrate that it has a full-time faculty dedicated to the programme. A requirement that a minimum of one-half the faculty be full-time with no (or severely limited) teaching assignments at other institutions would seem to be reasonable. One institution visited by the team obtains essentially all its general academic instruction from a nearby university. Such an arrangement is certainly workable and could have the advantages of engaging under-utilised faculty resources and avoiding duplication. Nevertheless, the academic faculty should assume full academic responsibility for the curriculum and should also have a commitment to developing the kinds of integrated curricula appropriate for a professionally oriented college. An institution should be required to demonstrate these points before receiving accreditation.

Open/distance learning and new modes of delivery

Open/distance learning can be an important means for Estonia to accommodate at least some of the increased demand and to extend learning opportunities to adult learners and communities throughout the country. Estonian leaders clearly recognise open/distance learning as a key means to ensure lifelong learning for all Estonia as envisioned in "Learning Estonia" supported by the President's Academic Council, the Education Forum, and the MoE. The Estonia's Education Scenarios 2015 describe a scenario in which:

> Lifelong learning has developed into a lifestyle, which is integrated with nearly all activities. Estonia's learning communities serve as pathfinders in the learning and teaching sphere, also in a global extent. [12]

A UNDP report on the Tiger Leap programme (see Chapter 3) outlined the challenge of

> "... an extension of the Tiger Leap aimed at ensuring an environment for the development of the whole of Estonia and for everyone's life-long learning, based on modern information technology. An open learning environment, extended communication opportunities and the free offer of services based on public and private interests would definitely create new opportunities for people, regions, businesses and for the state." [13]

Several Estonian higher education institutions are taking the lead in developing open/distance learning initiatives. The most active are the major public universities (University of Tartu, Tallinn Technological University, and Tallinn University of Educational Sciences) and two private institutions, Concordia International University and the Estonian Business School. Each of the public universities has established an "Open University" (Avatud ükooli). Open/distance learning is becoming an increasingly important means for the universities to provide higher education throughout Estonia, providing in-service training for teachers, university courses, and in some cases, full degree programmes.

The Phare Multi-country Programme for Distance Education has been an important catalyst for open/distance learning developments in Estonia and has been complementary to and supported the recent strategic developments initiated at both government and institution levels.[14]

Because of the diversity of open/distance learning programmes and services, and the new information communications technology (ICT) based modes of delivery, the growth in open/distance learning may be only partially reflected in official enrolment statistics. The data from the Statistical Office of Estonia on enrolments do not separately identify students enrolled in open/distance learning. However, the data show an increase of 140.4% in "evening" enrolments from 1994/95 to 1998/99 and a 23.9 decrease in "correspondence" enrolments. These data suggest that higher education in Estonia has shifted significantly away from the "correspondence" modes of extended learning of Soviet times to different modes of delivery and learning (see Table 21). [15]

The University of Tartu has embedded open/distance learning at the core of the university's revitalised mission of community service as a complement to the missions of teaching and research. While in its early history, the university had a strong mission of service to Estonia, that mission was largely abandoned in Soviet times. Now, the university's development plan calls for the university to be deeply engaged in improving the education, quality of life, and economy of every region of Estonia.

The initial efforts to carry out this mission focused on continuing professional education for adults with a goal of creating:

> "A system of lifelong study that would provide every member
> of society with access to education, irrespective of theirsocial
> or educational background, place of living or age, and would
> allow flexible switches between work and study, or unem-
> ployment, study and work." [16]

The adult and continuing education programmes range from courses preparing school leavers for university entrance examinations to professional development courses for university leavers. A particular emphasis is on professional development courses for teachers. The university has given particular attention to use of ICT-based study. Virtual teaching is seen as especially important because it provides a means for the institution to serve students throughout the country at times and places suitable them – without the need to travel to Tartu.

A number of initiatives focused on the community service mission are now the direct responsibility of the Vice-Rector for Open and Distance Learning. The activities of the Open University are organised, co-ordinated and supported by 4 centres:

- Distance Education Centre responsible for co-ordinating degree education and continuing education.

- Phare Distance Education Centre, responsible for developing and implementing new distance education methods.

- Regional Development Centre responsible for contacts between university faculties and counties, organising orientation days, lectures, conferences, seminars in counties and organising alumni activities.

- Multimedia Centre responsible for creating an IT-based learning environment, designing and printing research and study materials, and organising video, TV and audio-conferences.

The Open University offers a wide range of degree and non-degree programmes designed to meet highly diverse student needs. While the share of ICT-based learning has been increasing, the university makes an effort to retain a face-to-face element in most of its courses. Through the regional development centre, the university has developed an impressive network throughout Estonia of local centres and support services for students.

The Open University offers over 50 syllabi in all the faculties and colleges of the University. There were 13 diploma courses serving approximately 1 000 students as of the beginning of 2000. More than 900 students have been admitted to the 18 undergraduate programmes. There are 11 courses leading to a Master's degree, with approximately 300 students and 4 doctorate programmes, with 5 students. The total number of Open University students is circa 2 150 and they account for 16% of the 12 000 students of the University of Tartu.

The Phare Multi-country Programme supported the establishment of the Phare Distance Education Centre at the University of Tartu. Other sources of support include the State, local municipalities, NGOs, and the students themselves. [17]

The initiatives at the University of Tartu are the most extensive of any public university in Estonia. The OECD team recognises, however, that other universities, especially Tallinn Technical University and Tallinn University of Educational Sciences, are also playing leading roles in open/distance learning, especially in the application of ICT in new modes of course design, management, and delivery. These institutions have been deeply involved in the Phare Multi-Country Programme for Distance Education and other international projects of the Nordic Council and others. The national contact point for the Phare programme is located at Tallinn Technical University which operates as a satellite office of the Archimedes Foundation, the unit linked to the MoE, as described earlier in this chapter, that is responsible for national co-ordination of European programmes such as Socrates, Tempus and Leonardo.

Two open/distance learning centres have been established through the Phare programme, one at the University of Tartu, as described above, and the other is a joint venture between the Centre for Continuing Education at Tallinn Technical University, Tallinn University of Educational Sciences and the Estonian Business School. The Phare Centres have established advanced technological infrastructures and are using the Internet, the World Wide Web and ISDN-based video conferencing for course-delivery and co-ordination purposes.

The four Estonian institutions participating in the Phare programme have undertaken development of Open/Distance Learning during the last 3 to 4 years. This has been supported by the institutions' own strategic investments, the Phare programme, and others. Four courses were developed with Phare support in 1999: the Centre for Continuing Education at Tallinn Technical University developed a course on "Distance Education" and a course on "Environmental Law and Management"; Tallinn University of Educational Sciences developed a 5-module course on "Educational Technology"; and the Estonian Business School developed a diploma course on "Introduction to Business".

Tallinn University of Educational Sciences has been extensively involved in open/distance learning related to teacher education, including both traditional models of delivery and developing innovative applications of ICT (new Web-based courses, training of teachers in the use of new technology, etc.). The university is also participating in the Nordic-Baltic project on teacher training supported by the Nordic Council.

The OECD team strongly supports Estonia's intent to expand open/distance learning and other initiatives to improve access and opportunity making use of ICT and new modes of teaching and learning. Nevertheless, the team is concerned that Estonia must make further changes in the underlying policies that will be necessary to move open/distance learning – and the whole far broader commitment to lifelong learning – from the periphery to the core of the university and other institutions. The Law on Institutions of Higher Education, for example, makes no distinction between distance education delivery modes and traditional teaching formats. The basic quality assurance policies reflected in the Standard for Higher Education and regulations for institutional accreditation are strongly oriented to traditional institutions and modes of delivery. The accrediting process will be of limited use either in preventing serious abuse or promoting the highest quality new initiatives.

Current state financing policy also provides few incentives for long-term fundamental change. The criteria for allocation of funds to institutions emphasise traditional university disciplines and institution-based delivery. Several aspects of current policy have been important – although sometimes unintended – catalysts for the growth in open/distance learning. Serious limitations in state funding, the authority of institutions to accept paying students (under certain constraints), and university autonomy to make independent decisions on future directions, have combined to provide universities with strong incentives to expand open/distance learning to generate needed revenue. Expanding enrolments through open/distance learning has been a critical source of revenue to support increases in faculty salaries and basic improvements in university infrastructure. In addition to the availability of state funding for adult education (3% of the salary fund) has clearly fuelled demand for open/distance learning.

Nevertheless, the OECD team believes that Estonia must do far more than these somewhat "indirect" public policies to support open/distance learning and the goal of lifelong learning. Figure 13 summarises the kinds of policy changes that OECD countries are considering in the new environment. The philosophy underlying "Learning Estonia," and the progressive initiatives through Tiger Leap and the open/distance learning initiatives discussed above, strongly accord with the directions outlined on the "To" column of Figure 13. Nevertheless, State policies remain largely concentrated on the delivery system outlined in the "From" column.

The OECD urges Estonia to make a thorough review of all State laws, regulations, and other policies – especially policies on financing and quality assurance – to identify changes that will create the policy environment necessary to make open/distance learning and lifelong learning a reality, not just a vision.

Changes in teaching and learning within institutions

At several points in this report, the OECD has pointed to forward –thinking reports and initiatives in Estonia to transform teaching and learning – the need

Figure 13. **Summary of changes in tertiary education demand and delivery**

FROM:	TO:
Students defined largely by institutional attendance (public, private, proprietary, career or vocational).	Students defined largely by institutional attendance (public, private, proprietary, career or vocational).
Providers defined primarily in termsof traditional colleges and universi-ties and traditional on campus, class-room/lecture/recitation.	Providers defined primarily in termsof traditional colleges and universi-ties and traditional on campus, class-room/lecture/recitation.
Academic progress defined primarily in terms of traditional measures of academic time: clock hours, semester credit hours, semesters, academic years.	Academic progress defined primarily in terms of traditional measures of academic time: clock hours, semester credit hours, semesters, academic years.
Units of instruction defined primarily in terms of programmes and courses – each having a credit-hour value.	Units of instruction defined primarily in terms of programmes and courses – each having a credit-hour value.
Access defined in terms of students to gain financial and academic access to existing institutional providers (*e.g.*, institutions offering academic programmes and services in the traditional on-campus academic courses and programmes and related services).	Access defined in terms of students to gain financial and academic access to existing institutional providers (*e.g.*, institutions offering academic programmes and services in the traditional on-campus academic courses and programmes and related services).
Definition of a provider as an "institution" – encompassing not only the traditional core faculty responsibilities for advising and mentoring, curriculum, teaching, assessment or evaluation, and awarding credentials, but also core support services (*e.g.*, library, advising and counselling).	Definition of a provider as an "institution" – encompassing not only the traditional core faculty responsibilities for advising and mentoring, curriculum, teaching, assessment or evaluation, and awarding credentials, but also core support services (*e.g.*, library, advising and counselling).

Source: Aims C. McGuinness, Jr., State Postsecondary Education Sourcebook. Denver: Education Commission of the States, 1998, p. 9.

187

to a change to "learner" focus and to change from the passive, subject-matter, didactic instruction of the past to more active, integrated, inter-disciplinary approaches. From interviews and visits to schools and institutions in the course of the review, however, the OECD team gained the impression that the actual experience of most students in universities, colleges and other institutions is changing slowly. Students are still admitted to specialities and little progress seems to have been made in developing an understanding – much less agreement – on crosscutting issues such as general education. Despite the many positive features of the enhanced university research mission, it also may tend to lure faculty members away from teaching – especially if additional non-university (preferably private and international) support is not obtained for the research mission. Without institutional leadership and deliberate strategies such as those being pursued at several of the universities, the pressures on faculty members to strengthen traditional scholarship in the disciplines will draw energy away from application, inter-disciplinary work, and community service.

These are issues that universities throughout the world face. There are no easy answers especially in a situation in which Estonia is implementing the important step of re-establishing the research mission of its universities. The OECD team is especially concerned that only limited efforts are now being made within universities to develop and renew faculty resources – especially in terms of faculty skills in using new modes of instructional delivery and pedagogy. New skills in academic leadership and the use of internal and external incentives are needed to shift faculty attention from the challenges of meeting day-to-day obligations of research and lectures to broader questions about the future of teaching and learning. One of the promising spin-offs of open-distance learning, for example, is that it provides a venue for at least some faculty members to learn new approaches and provides the added incentive of the potential for additional funding.

As stressed in Chapter 3, it will be difficult for universities to lead in preparing the next generation of teachers for basic and secondary education if the teaching and learning paradigm within does not change. The OECD team urges Estonia to give higher priority to policies at the State and institutional levels to stimulate change in teaching and learning within higher education institutions as an essential pre-condition for a stronger university role in preparing the next generation of teachers and school leaders.

Financing, governance and accountability

The issues of financing, governance and accountability, as observed by the OECD team, are inter-related. Financing policy (how the state allocates funds to institutions, student fees, and related issues) is one of the most important ways that the State influences the directions of the higher education system. Governance determines authority and responsibility for allocation, management, and utilisation of resources. The OECD team heard repeated calls for changes in current financing policies. The following is a summary of points made in the course of the review and suggestions for next steps from the perspective of the OECD team.

The costs of meeting the demand for higher education and other priorities such as the need to develop a competitive research infrastructure are outstripping any realistic possibility for the State to finance the system under current policy assumptions. Certainly increased State funding should be a priority, but how higher education is financed may be as important as the level of funding.

Estonia has moved to a system that is increasingly dependent on student fees – more because of the force of economic realities than because of a conscious policy choice. The issue of increasing student fees is a major source of tensions in countries throughout the world and the nature of the debate depends greatly on a country's history and culture. In Estonia, student fees are already a significant source of revenue for most institutions since institutions are authorised to enrol fee-paying students in addition to State-financed student numbers. As State financing has been severely limited, student fee revenue has been essential for institutions to improve faculty salaries, infrastructure and otherwise improve quality. A major motivation for expanding open/distance learning is that it can generate revenue from student fees. The growing private sector is largely financed by student fees (except in the case that the State may finance student numbers in selected accredited study programmes).

The OECD team is concerned that Estonia faces a serious policy question regarding equity in student financing. The criteria for gaining access to State-funded student places are based on academic merit (a policy common to most OECD countries) but without consideration of a student's economic circumstances and ability to pay. As the number of State funded student places is necessary limited, a growing number of academically qualified students must pay student fees. This leaves a sharp divide between those who pay no fees and those who must pay full tuition costs – a divide that does not reflect the true differences in academic merit or the potential benefit of each graduate to state priorities.

The OECD team recognises that Estonia has a system of student loans and the state will "forgive" loans of students undertaking certain kinds of employment (*e.g.*, working in rural schools). The team, however, did not get the impression that the conditions for repayment reflect differences in students' economic status. According to the law on student support being prepared in the Ministries of Education and Finance, the proposal to support students whose income in the last 6 months is below the threshold annually determined by the Government. The draft law will be submitted to the Government in autumn 2000.

The financing policies also seem to be barriers to efficient improvements and the alignment of public resources with developing State priorities. High demand study programmes (such as law, business, foreign languages, and information technology) can generate substantially more revenue than low demand programmes (most often in the physical sciences and fields associated with former times). Other disciplines or professions (such as the arts and humanities and education) may also be able to generate fewer student fees because of comparatively low wages in the labour market. Presumably, some institutions will be able to generate significant revenue, while others, especially those in rural areas and small towns, will not be able to.

In theory, the State allocations among disciplines and professions change over time based on State priorities and student demand. Nevertheless, in Estonia, as in other countries, these changes tend to lag behind the changing market because of the need to avoid rapid disruptions in institutional or programme funding. The result can be an increasing misalignment between State priorities and the actual allocations.

Institutions can often manage these internal imbalances, provided they have the necessary autonomy and management flexibility and expertise – and, support from their faculties. The issue for the State, however, is that these institutional decisions may not always align with State priorities. The OECD team heard reports, however, of significant differences among institutions in both their authority and management capability to handle these internal tensions. The autonomy of universities provides these institutions with substantially more authority to manage resources than vocational or applied higher education institutions, but some universities are clearly more experienced than others.

Even if Estonia maintained its current financing policies, the OECD recommends that priority be given to developing the management capabilities at all higher education institutions. As suggested earlier in the discussion of consolidating smaller entities to form larger institutions or complexes, it is important for Estonia to develop entities that have the potential to achieve needed improvements in resource utilisation. Whether they will be able to obtain these improvements will depend on leadership and management capability.

Another concern heard by the OECD team is that, despite the impressive forward thinking regarding "Learning Estonia," at the time of the review Estonia did not have an agreed upon strategy plan or public agenda for the future of higher education. Because of the largely beneficial actions to increase university autonomy and decentralise the system, the mechanisms and staff capability to provide overall strategic direction and system co-ordination are underdeveloped. Lacking such an agreed – upon public agenda, the Government's policies and mechanism for allocating State funding establish – by default – the policy incentives to which the system responds. As suggested above in the discussion of open/distance learning and lifelong learning, there appears to be a misalignment between present State policies and the policy directions implied in "Learning Estonia."

The challenge for Estonia – as it is for all OECD Member countries – is to establish the means for nation-wide strategic direction for higher education – while at the same time supporting a highly decentralised, flexible and responsive network of institutions. Higher education is perhaps the most important national resource for developing the human and intellectual resources of a small country to compete in the global economy. In the past – and especially in Soviet times – governments would use centralised control and regulation to establish directions. Throughout the world, governments are moving away from direct ownership and control of institutions to a new governmental role emphasising policy leadership and overall supervision and the use of financial incentives and performance-based accountability requirements.

The leaders in Estonia clearly recognise and support these changes. From the discussions during the review, the OECD team senses that a number of practical issues must be resolved in order to make progress. For example, as mentioned earlier, some of the fiscal and management flexibility now available to the universities should be extended to all higher education institutions – provided they meet certain preconditions.

To balance this decentralisation, the OECD team recommends that Estonia use a combination of changes in financing, governance, and accountability policies to ensure that the system responds to a strategic agenda for the future of Estonia. Alternatives could include:

- A stronger role of the MoE in shaping and gaining consensus around a public agenda for the future of higher education in Estonia, and linking this agenda to State financing and accountability policies. Such an agenda should link the vision of "Learning Estonia" to concrete policy changes in financing and other areas over a multi-year period. The MoE

Strategic Platform for 2000-2004 represents an important step in this direction.

- A new financing policy that would provide for a sharing of the cost of higher education between the State and all students, target State resources to address public priorities, and ensure equitable access of qualified students to study programmes.

State investment funds designed to support initiatives that move the nation toward the vision of "Learning Estonia," such as:

- Renewing human resources – faculty members, deans and support personnel – throughout the higher education system (retraining of existing personnel as well as developing the next generation).

- Strengthening the capacity in selected high priority fields for universities to compete for research funding from EU and other international funding sources.

- Providing incentives for institutions to improve quality and realign resources.

- Providing incentives for stronger collaboration among institutions across all education sectors in meeting regional economic and human resource development needs and in reforming the nation's education system.

- Continuing to develop a nation-wide network for open distance learning.

- Multiyear "compacts" between the Government and each public institution designed to strengthen institutional strategic planning and direction, increasing the stability of funding, and providing for clearer public reporting and accountability. The OECD team recognises that this may not be possible in current circumstances. The problem for the MoE is that the allocations depend on the annual budget. Also, the universities would probably not be prepared to sign contracts based on the current base costings. Multi-year contracts would be possible in a more stable system.

- Establishing a new framework for public accountability at both the system and institutional levels – including periodic public reporting on performance. This system should include indicators for measuring performance of the system (*e.g.*, progress in meeting the vision of "Learning Estonia and in addressing the nation's major educational, economic and social priorities), and indicators for institutional performance (such as alignment of resources with mission and responsiveness to public priorities).

In summary, the OECD team agrees with the MoE that financing higher education is a critical policy issue facing Estonia. The issues of financing cannot be easily separated from issues of governance and accountability.

Summary of recommendations

Develop a more diversified higher education system by consolidating and strengthening the quality and efficiency of non-university institutions to create a network of "colleges" throughout the country. Such a network is essential to meet the growing demands for student access and the nation's future labour market needs. Given the diversity of the country, a combination of institutional approaches, including both independent and university-linked institutions is likely to be the most appropriate strategy.

- Give particular attention to the co-ordination among institutions, centres, branches and other entities serving the same municipality or region. Co-ordination will be especially important between higher education institutions in each region and regional centres for in-service teacher training mentioned in Chapter 3 and developing regional training centres related to vocational education and training discussed in Chapter 4.

- Utilise financing policy to provide incentives for promoting regional co-ordination and to ensure that students, employers, or communities receive the highest quality, most cost-effective service.

Continue to strengthen the provisions of the Standard for Higher Education and accreditation requirements related to both study programmes and institutions. As a basic requirement, no study programme should be accredited unless an institution can demonstrate that it has a full-time faculty dedicated to the programme. A requirement that a minimum of one-half the faculty be full-time with no (or severely limited) teaching assignments at other institutions would seem to be reasonable.

Continue to expand open/distance learning and other initiatives to improve access and opportunity making use of ICT and new modes of teaching and learning.

Make a thorough review of all State laws, regulations, and other policies – especially policies on financing and quality assurance – to identify changes necessary to move open-distance learning – and the whole far broader commitment to lifelong learning – from the periphery to the core of the university and other institutions.

Place higher priority on policies at the State and institutional levels to stimulate change in teaching and learning within higher education institutions as an essential pre-condition for a stronger university role in preparing the next generation of teachers and school leaders. As stressed in Chapter 3, it will be difficult for universities to lead in preparing the next generation of teachers for basic and secondary education if the teaching and learning paradigm within does not change.

Continue to pursue changes in the financing of higher education recognising this as one of the critical policy issues facing Estonia. Recognise that financing cannot be easily separated from issues of governance and accountability.

Continue to pursue policy directions to decentralise institutional management and redefine the role of the MoE toward policy leadership and overall supervision. Extend to all higher education institutions some of the fiscal and management flexibility now available to the universities provided they meet certain preconditions regarding quality and management capability.

Place high priority on developing the management capabilities at all higher education institutions as a precondition for effective decentralisation.

Pursue a co-ordinated set of policy changes in financing, governance, and accountability policies to balance decentralisation, and to ensure that the system responds to a strategic agenda for the future of Estonia. Alternatives could include:

- A stronger role of the MoE in shaping and gaining consensus around a public agenda for the future of higher education in Estonia, and linking this agenda to State financing and accountability policies. Such an agenda should link the vision of "Learning Estonia" to concrete policy changes in financing and other areas over a multiyear period. The MoE Strategic Platform for 2000-2004 represents an important step in this direction.

- A new financing policy that would provide for a sharing of the cost of higher education between the State and all students, target State resources to address public priorities, and ensure equitable access of qualified students to student programmes.

State investment funds designed to support initiatives that move the nation toward the vision of "Learning Estonia," such as:

- Renewing human resources – faculty members, deans and support personnel – throughout the higher education system (retraining of existing personnel as well as developing the next generation).

- Strengthening the capacity in selected high priority fields for universities to compete for research funding from EU and other international funding sources.

- Providing incentives for institutions to improve quality and realign resources.

- Providing incentives for stronger collaboration among institutions across all education sectors in meeting regional economic and human resource development needs and in reforming the nation's education system.

- Continuing to develop a nation-wide network for open-distance learning.

- Multiyear "compacts" between the Government and each public institution designed to strengthen institutional strategic planning and direction, increasing the stability of funding, and providing for clearer public reporting and accountability.

- Establishing a new framework for public accountability at both the system and institutional levels – including periodic public reporting on performance. This system should include indicators for measuring performance of the system (*e.g.*, progress in meeting the vision of "Learning Estonia and in addressing the nation's major educational, economic and social priorities), and indicators for institutional performance (such as alignment of resources with mission and responsiveness to public priorities).

Notes

1. Ministry of Education, Estonia Academic Recognition Centre, Higher Education in Estonia, Second Edition, Tallinn 2000, p. 6.

2. Academic Recognition Centre, pp. 8-23.

2. Eurydice, pp. 27-31.

4. Joint declaration of the European Ministers of Education, The European Higher Education Area, Bologna, June 19, 1999.

5. Academic Recognition Centre, pp. 22-23.

6. Eurydice, p. 28.

7. Jüri Engelbrecht, Scientific Development in a Small Country, Estonia: Candidate for Membership in the European Union. Tallinn: International Business Book, 1998-99, pp. 175.185. This sector draws extensively on this article by Professor Jüri Engelbrecht, President of the Estonian Academy of Sciences. Professor Engelbrecht provided the OECD team with an overview of Estonian science policy during the review.

8. World Bank, Task Force on Higher Education and Society, Higher Education in Developing Countries: Peril and Promise. Washington: The World Bank, 2000, pp. 26-28.

9. Statistical Office of Estonia, Haridus 1998/99, Table 5.1,Tallinn 1999, p. 184.

10. Ministry of Education, Strategy Platform, 2000-2004, Short Survey, Spring 2000, summary compiled by: Heli Aru Counsellor to the Minister and translated from Estonian, 30 March 2000.

11. Jaak Aaviskoo, Rector of Tartu University, presentation at the Salzburg Seminar on Higher Education, April 2000.

12. K, Loogma, R. Rein Ruubel, V. Ruus, E, Sarv, R. Vilu, "Estonia's Education Scenarios 2015, Tallinn, 1998, p. 23.

13. UNDP, Tiger Leap into the XXIst Century, Tallinn, 1999, Chapter 3.

14. European Training Foundation, Programme Compendium, Phare Multi-Country Programme for Distance Education, 1999, pp. 15-17.

15. Statistical Office of Estonia, Haridus 1998/99, Table 5.1,Tallinn 1999, p. 184. Note: ** Increase from 1995/96 to 1998/99.

16. Teat Seen and One Val, The Policy of the University of Tartu for Continuing Education," p. 2.

17. European Training Foundation, Programme Compendium, Phare Multi-Country Programme for Distance Education, 1999, pp. 15-17.

Chapter 6

From Forward Thinking to Action

Progress in reform

From a comparative perspective, Estonia has made impressive progress since independence in its journey toward an open, democratic society and market economy, with a capacity to thrive and compete in the global economy. This progress is reflected in:

- The basic legal structure now in place for all levels of the system pre-school education, general education, vocational education, universities and applied higher education, private schools, research and development, and adult education.

- The national curriculum for basic and secondary education.

- New assessment and testing policies and other initiatives to improve quality and accountability.

- Access to technology (ICT) throughout the education system.

- Reforms in vocational education designed to strengthen the knowledge and skills of students to enter the labour market and to strengthen links with social partners and regional economic development.

- Significant progress in broadening the mission of the universities to encompass strong, internationally competitive initiatives in teaching and research and nation-wide initiatives in services to regions, municipalities, and professionals.

- Initial steps in shaping a more diverse higher education system – including a developing non-university "college" sector – to accommodate escalating demand and the changing needs of the labour market.

- Important developments in open/distance learning demonstrating the potential for reaching target populations and regions through new modes of teaching and learning and for making lifelong learning accessible to all Estonians.

- Significant pilot and demonstration projects – many supported by the European Union, the Open Estonia Foundation, bilateral agreements with Nordic countries, and other sources.

Areas for further improvement

Despite this progress and many positive, promising aspects of the Estonian education system, the OECD identified several crosscutting themes reflecting areas for further progress.

Moving from forward-thinking to strategy and action

The OECD team was especially impressed with the forward-thinking about the future of Estonia and the critical role that education must play in developing the knowledge, skills, and attitudes of all Estonians in the global knowledge economy. There is clearly a deepening interest around the vision of "Learning Estonia", articulated by the President's Academic Council, the Estonian Education Forum, and by the MoE's Strategy statements.

The OECD team was concerned at the time of the review that, despite the impressive forward-thinking, Estonia was having difficulty in reaching closure on debates about strategy and in agreeing on concrete policy actions that would move the system toward the vision of "Learning Estonia". Furthermore, the process for developing these strategies appeared to the review team not to have included the broad public debate and engagement of the Republic's employers and other social partners. Since the OECD review, the Ministry of Education has co-ordinated the preparation of an Education Strategy document for 2000-2004, which was submitted to the Government in September. Various social partners have contributed to the document. Ambiguities and barriers in the current system of governance and finance appeared to provide few incentives for schools, municipalities, institutions, and other entities to make the difficult decisions necessary to improve quality while reducing costs. Basic policy mechanisms to guide and sustain systemic change appear to be lacking at the level of the

Ministry, across ministries addressing similar issues, within the major sectors, and at the regional and local levels.

It is, therefore, especially encouraging to the team that the MoE and the Riigikogu either have taken – or will soon take – action on specific steps over the next four or five years to address important unresolved policy questions. The MoE Strategy Platform 2000-2004 includes a realistic assessment of the challenges facing Estonia – an assessment that highlights a number of the concerns identified in the course of the OECD review. It then sets forth policy actions to be taken in the short-term to move the long-term agenda forward. The recommendations in earlier chapters of this report expressed OECD support for a number of specific actions in the Strategy Platform.

The OECD team's concerns remain, however, about the extent to which the nation's private sector – employers and other social partners – are engaged in the discourse and are fully committed to the steps necessary to develop "Learning Estonia". The UNDP report, Tiger Leap into the XXIst Century underscores the point that the values of "Learning Estonia" must pervade not just the formal education system but all dimensions of Estonia's society and economy – all regions, ethnic groups, business and industry, government, and other social institutions. Estonia's political and education leaders recognise that without broad public support and without the supporting infrastructure of social partners and NGOs, it will be difficult to achieve long-term, sustained improvement. The OECD wishes to reinforce the efforts of these leaders to broaden and deepen the public engagement in the issue. Important strategies include using the news media (print and ICT-based) for creating and sustaining a public understanding and commitment to needed changes.

Moving from a system focused on top achievers to one engaging all learners

Estonia must develop all its human resources in order to function as an open, democratic society, and to be competitive in the world economy. The danger is in growing disparities in the quality of education for different segments of the Estonian population in a manner similar to the scenario of "Estonia of Market Education and Elite Schools". The potential problems are evident in:

- The tendency of both the National Curriculum, testing and assessment to emphasise subject matter and knowledge appropriate for those intending to pursue university-level education and to give insufficient attention to the diversity of student learning needs.

- Continuing differences among secondary general education schools (between "elite" gymnasiums and "regular" secondary schools, or between private and public schools).

- Differences in expectations and resources (such as access to ICT) between secondary general and secondary vocational schools.

- Disparities between urban and rural schools, and among municipalities and regions depending on the severity of economic and social dislocation.

- Differences between Estonian-language and non-Estonian language schools.

An even greater challenge remains in serving the needs of the Republic's adult population. With declining birth rates and other demographic changes, Estonia will be heavily dependent on the knowledge and skills of the existing adult workforce well into the next century. Estonia has a high adult literacy rate, but the adult population is seriously in need of opportunities for retraining in order to function in the new economy. Specific areas for improvement – most of which are included in the MoE Strategy Platform – include:

- Evaluating the extent to which the specific requirements and items of both the National Curriculum and testing/assessment instruments align with the underlying "learner centred philosophy of the National Curriculum."

- Continuing to diversify secondary education – especially in strengthening the general education components of vocational education and increasing the opportunities for practical application and orientation to the labour market in gymnasiums.

- Addressing the problem of small rural schools.

- Strengthening the vocational education system.

- Ensuring access to ICT throughout the education system – but especially in secondary vocational education and to less advantaged municipalities and regions.

- Developing a system for adult education and retraining.

- Elaborating policies regarding student financing at the tertiary education level.

- Continuing progress regarding the non-Estonian language population and ethnic minorities.

Aligning national policy and implementation with the underlying "learner-centred" philosophy of learning Estonia

Estonia has made excellent progress since the 1990s to develop and implement a new National Curriculum, and new testing and assessment requirements. As emphasised in Chapter 2, however, the OECD team is concerned that a gap remains between the philosophy and intent of the new policies and the more detailed implementation. The OECD team is especially concerned about the need to give more attention in the next revision of the National Curriculum to the integration of subject matter with practical application and problem-solving, interdisciplinary curricula, and sensitivity to more diverse student and learner needs.

Of broader concern is the impact of a strong, centrally testing and assessment system on the kind of bottom-up, participatory school-based initiative that Estonia has been seeking to develop since the early days of reform. The danger is that the pressures on schools and teachers to achieve strong results on tests will only reinforce the passive, "compliant" teaching and learning that the reforms seek to discourage. This potential problem is not unique to Estonia. Several OECD countries are implementing reforms emphasising higher standards and "high-stakes" testing and assessment. A key to the success of these reforms is the development of strong support networks (in-service education, curricular materials, and technical assistance to support school change). The OECD team was especially impressed by the extent to which Estonia recognises the need for such support as illustrated by the networks developed from the "Distinctive Schools," and the current quality schools initiative. The question remaining for the OECD team is whether the capacity exists to provide the necessary support for school-level change on a systemic basis throughout Estonia. For example, in Chapter 2, the team raises concerns about whether the inspectorate function of the MoE related county offices had moved away from the practices of earlier times (using the curriculum as a device for control) to practices consistent with the new paradigm.

Developing the human resources of the education system

Continuing progress on education reform will depend fundamentally on the capacity of teachers to adapt, learn, and embrace new approaches to teaching

201

and learning. Estonia has initiated at central level significant reforms and has established a number of promising pilot projects and initiatives related to in-service training for teachers, training of school principals, reform of teacher education curricula, and other important reform elements. The OECD team's assessment, however, is that these elements do not yet add up to a co-ordinated, sustainable strategy by Estonia to achieve systemic change. The human resource development needs are at every level of the system as stressed in each of the chapters of this report. Especially difficult challenges remain in developing the next generation of faculty for universities and the non-university higher education sector in order to accommodate escalating student demand.

Achieving more with the same resources used differently

The OECD mission heard consistently that funding is a problem. This is not so much a problem of the total allocation, although of course this could be increased. The problem is more one of making more efficient use of the existing resources. Without significant improvements in the efficient use of resources, Estonia will not be able to achieve its goals for improving the quality of education for all Estonians. The MoE clearly recognises this challenge as reflected in the efforts to consolidate or merge small institutions, create larger school complexes, and other strategies to achieve economies of scale and improve quality. Because of the serious limitations in available human resources – teachers, school directors – it is especially important to avoid further dispersion of these resources. The initiatives to decentralise responsibility for school management could increase incentives for efficient resource utilisation, but a strong commitment to training of school directors will be necessary to make these reforms effective.

Balancing decentralisation and institutional autonomy with a new role for MoE

Decentralisation of the governance and management of schools and institutions is consistent with progressive policy developments throughout the world. At the higher education level, university autonomy has clearly enabled these institutions to improve quality, diversify revenue, improve internal management, and respond more effectively to regional and national priorities. Decentralising governance and financial management of other higher education institutions would be an important step to improve these institutions.

It is important to balance institutional autonomy and decentralisation with a new role for the MoE in overall policy leadership and co-ordination, and in ensuring accountability. The MoE has been moving away from the historical role of operating and controlling schools and institutions – primarily by detailed control of inputs – to a broader role of supervision and monitoring of system and institutional performance. As suggested in Chapter 4, the OECD team recommends that the MoE undertake a broader role in higher education strategic planning, quality assurance, and accountability. Recognising the reality that resources at the level of the MoE will be severely constrained, it is important to focus on a limited number of priority functions. Four MoE roles will be increasingly important:

- **Developing and sustaining a broad public consensus on the fundamental goals for education in Estonia – "Learning Estonia".** As stressed above, more effort must be devoted to employers and other social partners, the media, and, the general public in support of change and improvement.

- **Promoting co-ordination across the Government of functions that relate to education.** This co-ordination is important not only for functions specifically identified as education (such as vocational education and training), but also functions and initiatives related to children, families, health, information technology infra-structure, and public administration reform that have an impact on education policy.

- **Promoting public accountability by analysing and reporting on the performance of schools, institutions, and the system as a whole.** To carry out this function, the MoE will need a significantly improved information system and analytic capacity, and a system of indicators and benchmarks for monitoring performance from an international comparative perspective.

- **Continuing to develop strategic alliances with NGOs, employers and International Organisations to support and sustain reform.** NGOs and international sponsors have been critical to most of the significant education reforms in Estonia over the past decade and will continue to be essential in the future. The MoE plays an important role in facilitating co-ordination among these multiple initiatives and in aligning its own programmes (for example, in-service teacher training) with these initiatives.

Conclusion

Estonia is on an exciting, challenging journey to create a dynamic, innovative, responsive, learner-centred education system. The nation's leaders recognise the daunting challenge as a small country to develop a distinctive role in the

203

global knowledge economy and of overcoming the legacy of the past and severe economic constraints to realise the vision of "Learning Estonia". The OECD team believes that the Government's strategies for reform are fundamentally sound. The team is confident that – with perseverance – Estonia will continue to make steady progress toward its goals.

Selected bibliography

AAVIKSOO, J., "The University of Tartu," presentation at the 2000 Salzburg CEPES/ UNESCO Conference.

Council of Europe Press, Secondary Education in Estonia, 1996.

Estonian Academy of Science, Science and Society: Charting the Future, International Conference, Conference Abstracts, December 1998, Tallinn, 1999.

Estonian Institute for Future Studies, Estonia's Development Scenarios Until Year 2010, Tallinn, 1997.

Estonian National Observatory, National Report on VET System, Updated March 1999.

European Commission, Regular Report from the Commission on Progress Toward Accession: Estonia – October 13, 1999.

European Commission, Eurydice, Supplement to the Study on the Structures of the Education and Initial Training Systems in the EU. The Situation in Estonia, Latvia, Lithuania, Slovenia and Cyprus, 1999.

European Training Foundation, Phare Multi-Country Programme for Distance Learning, Programme Compendium, European Training Foundation, 1999.

International Business Handbook, 1998/99, Estonia: Candidate for Membership in the European Union, 1999.

LOOGMA, K., RUUBEL, R, RUUS, V, SARV, E, VILU, R, Estonia's Education Scenarios 2015, Tallinn 1998.

OECD (2000), OECD Economic Surveys: Baltic States, Paris.

Open Estonia Foundation, Annual Reports, Tallinn, 1995, 1996, 1997, 1998.

Republic of Estonia, Ministry of Economic Affairs, Estonian Economy in 1998, and Estonian Economy, The Quarter in Review 3/1999, Tallinn.

Republic of Estonia, Ministry of Education, Academic Recognition Information Centre, Higher Education in Estonia, second edition, editors Gunnar Vaht, Maiki Udam, Kadri Kütt, Tallinn, 1999.

Republic of Estonia, President of the Republic's Academic Council, "A Learning Estonia, report to the Riigikogu, Tartu, Tallinn, 19 February 1998.

Seene, T and Valkm, A , The Policy of the University of Tartu for Continuing Education, Tartu, 1999.

Statistical Office of Estonia, Haridus 1998/99, and 1997/98, Tallinn, 1999 and 2000.

United Nations Development Program, Human Development Report 1998, 1999, Tallinn.

United Nations Development Program , The Estonian Tiger Leap into the 21st Century, Tallinn, 1999.

UNICEF, The MONEE Project, Regional Monitoring Report, Women in Transition: A Summary, Florence, 1999.

UNICEF, The MONEE Project CEE/CIS/Baltics, Regional Monitoring Report No. Education for All?, Report No. 5, Florence, 1999.

World Bank, Task Force on Higher Education and Society, Higher Education in Developing Countries: Peril and Promise. Washington, DC: The World Bank, 2000.

OECD PUBLICATIONS, 2, rue André-Pascal, 75775 PARIS CEDEX 16
PRINTED IN FRANCE
(14 2001 04 1P) ISBN 92-64-18607-7 – No. 51771 2001